T0198525

The
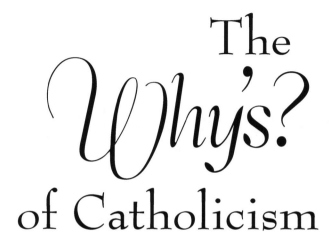 Why's?
of Catholicism

Vincent J. Heaton Jr.

WESTBOW
PRESS®
A DIVISION OF THOMAS NELSON
& ZONDERVAN

WestBow Press books may be ordered through booksellers or by contacting:

WestBow Press
A Division of Thomas Nelson & Zondervan
1663 Liberty Drive
Bloomington, IN 47403
www.westbowpress.com
1 (866) 928-1240

The New American Bible: Washington, DC: United States Conference of Catholic Bishops, 2002.

ISBN: 978-1-9736-6767-4 (sc)
ISBN: 978-1-9736-6769-8 (hc)
ISBN: 978-1-9736-6768-1 (e)

Library of Congress Control Number: 2019908814

Print information available on the last page.

WestBow Press rev. date: 04/21/2020

Dedication

This book evolved over many years of teaching Religious Education to junior high school students. My inspiration to teach originated with a call by the Holy Spirit after I started questioning what and how my own children were being instructed in our first parish. I understood the Holy Spirit wanted me to quit questioning, get off the sidelines, and get involved. That was well over three decades ago.

I never would have considered teaching Religious Education had it not been for the quality of education I received in the Catholic schools I was blessed to attend from kindergarten through college. Equally important to my faith formation was the "home tutoring" and "faith by example" provided by my parents, Vince and Eileen Heaton. Despite bringing fifteen children into this world, they always prioritized and invested in a good Catholic education for each one of us and then complimented that formal instruction with every-day, real life "walking the talk".

My parents led us and taught us by example. My father's strong faith, morals and character, set the bar high for me and served as a template for how I should behave in all facets of my life: personal, professional, social, and religious. My mother lived and continues to live her faith every single day by attending daily mass and she taught Religious Education at the elementary level for years. Now more than half of my siblings and several of their spouses teach Religious Education. She instilled in us a thirst for knowledge about our faith and a conviction to live that faith. Together my parents taught us the value of prayer and to place our trust in God, through good times and challenging ones.

Any good that might come from this book and any persons' life it might positively influence, is a gift from the Holy Spirit and my beautiful parents.

Gratefully,

Vincent J. Heaton, Jr

Introduction

This is a compilation of just some of the questions raised by young adults preparing for the Sacrament of Confirmation. I tried to answer each one of these questions based on using authoritative sources I understood to be consistent with the teachings of the Holy Catholic Church and the Holy See. When I could not find an authoritative Catholic position for a particular question or aspect of a question, I clearly indicate I am responding with personal opinion.

In my Religious Education classes I challenge my students to take the time to understand what being Catholic means, especially in those dogmatic areas that are unique to Catholicism. My objectives are to get them to think more about their faith and to understand the "whys" behind each dogmatic position. It is not enough to know what the Catholic Church's positions are in all these important areas of dogma. The key is to understand the basis, the "whys" for these positions to more objectively and knowledgably come to accept and believe in them. As Confirmed Catholics, we re-commit ourselves to the faith we were initiated into at Baptism. We are also completing or sealing what was started in Baptism and receive a special grace from the Holy Spirit, similar to the grace the apostles received on Pentecost. As Confirmed Catholics we commit to learning more about our faith, to developing an even closer relationship with Christ and, to going out and living or practicing that faith (evangelizing)…every day…to the best of our ability.

To stimulate that thinking process, I start each class by raising questions related to the lesson for that class. I then answer those questions through the course of the lesson. I make it clear I am raising these questions NOT to get them to doubt their faith, but rather, to think more about their faith and understand WHY we as Catholics believe what we believe. My hope was that this approach would strengthen their beliefs and would help better position them to explain their faith to others.

On the second to last class of each block (every five weeks we would mix up the classes so students would experience multiple catechists and their respective approaches over the course of the year), each student had to leave me at least one (often times I would get multiple) anonymous questions they had about their Catholic faith or about any other faith related question they may have had. I then researched each question using good Catholic references to answer their questions. This is a compilation of a selection of some of those questions and my answers.

My answers tend to be more detailed and in-depth as I am answering these questions with the expectation that these questions will come up again in high school or in college. I am writing these answers and including what I believe to be great sources for high school, college and all age Catholics, Christians and to all who are looking for answers to their faith related questions.

I respond to the immediate question raised but regularly address related questions one might have with my more in-depth, more detailed answers, with the hope and expectation this will be helpful to a wider range of ages from teens to adults who might have similar questions as they challenge their own beliefs and basis for those beliefs. I also use this broader response approach for often the basis for these questions could be interpreted multiple ways or were not always clear to me.

I thank the two parishes that gave me the privilege of teaching Religious Education for the last thirty plus years: Sacred Heart Parish in Lombard, Il, and St. Michael Parish in Wheaton, Il. I have learned much more about my faith in this process than I believe I have helped individual students learn about their faith. I pray that those students I was privileged to teach, came away more knowledgeable about their faith, stronger as a result, and more excited to continue deepening their relationship with Jesus Christ.

Sincerely,

Vincent J. Heaton, Jr.

Acknowledgements

There are many who invaluably enabled, encouraged, contributed, supported and facilitated the creation and publication of this book. I am indebted and most thankful to all these co-contributors and to the many others I have not specifically referenced here.

First, I thank each one of my students who challenged me with their good questions of faith over my three plus decades of teaching Religious Education. Your questions helped me dig deeper into the Church's positions, into the rich oral and written tradition of the Catholic Church, and into the basis for these positions. Your questions helped me deepen my own faith, understanding, and confidence in the solid foundation for these positions. I am quite confident that this process helped your fellow students and will help countless others who will read these questions and answers and strengthen their own understanding, their own faith.

I thank the many Pastors, RE Directors and staff personnel of Sacred Heart Parish in Lombard, Il and St. Michael Parish in Wheaton, Il who encouraged and supported me as a catechist. Both parishes have a strong commitment to providing a meaningful faith formation experience for all age groups and for all those seeking to better come to know and be in relationship with Jesus Christ.

A very special thanks to the Very Reverend John Balluff of the Joliet Diocesan Office for his guidance, advice and editorial improvement suggestions. His inputs significantly raised the overall quality, accuracy and caliber of this publication.

I thank all the good people at Westbow Press who helped me through the whole publishing process for me as a true rookie who had and still has so very much to learn. Their collective, collaborative efforts made this very rough idea become a blessed reality.

Finally, and most importantly, I thank my beautiful and loving wife and the mother of our seven children, my Madelyn Marie, for her support, patience and understanding over my more than three decades of teaching and over the countless hours of researching and responding to all my student's faith questions. She alone knows how seriously I took each question and why I invested so heavily in this process. I did not save all the questions raised and my related responses over the years, but those I did save numbered well over five hundred. Without her help and support, not only would this book never have happened, but I never would even have had the opportunity to plant seeds of faith and understanding in so many young adults. She put the voice and the words to the Holy Spirit's message of encouragement.

Sincerely,

Vincent J. Heaton Jr.

1. How do I know there is a God, that he made the world, or that he made me? And, how do I know Jesus is the Son of that God?

Volumes have been written to address these same questions, but I will do my best to provide summary insight and direction. This effort to respond reminds me of the story I heard regarding a college final exam for an advanced philosophy course. It was customary for final exams, for courses like this, for the students to be given "blue books" which are simply booklets of blank lined pages with a blue front and back cover. Typically, you would be given multiple essay questions and you would endeavor to write as much as you could, as profoundly as you could, hoping you accurately covered all the critical points the professor was expecting for each area of question. Well, as this story goes, the professor hands out several blue books per student, since this exam represented one hundred percent of their grade. He then simply wrote on the board, not multiple final exam questions, but rather one question, and a question with only one word. The question was, "Why?". The class had ninety minutes to organize and then capture their thoughts in a maximum of three blue books. The students began pondering this simple but hugely comprehensive philosophical question and then started writing furiously. Most of the class stayed writing and filling in their blue books right up until the end of the ninety-minute period. However, the whole class was perplexed when one student, generally known as bright, stood up after only a few minutes, barely long enough to write his name on the front of the blue book and turned in a lone blue book.

As the story goes, this student received the highest grade in the class and he only wrote a two-word response to the final exam question, which was in fact a question of his own. The student wrote, "Why not?".

So, unlike the "A" student in the story, while I am tempted to respond to these questions with a simple "trust me, your parents, your pastor or the pope", I will do my best to address these in a more detailed but still high level and hopefully helpful manner.

For centuries man has sought answers to key questions regarding the origin of our universe and of mankind. Some have gone even more primal and questioned if they really exist or just exist in their own mind. Yes, heavy philosophical thoughts.

Over these centuries our abilities, our knowledge and our resource base has expanded significantly to help us better address these fundamental questions. However, despite this extensive resource and experience base, not all questions can be empirically answered. Some require a "leap of faith". But I would suggest not a blind leap of faith but a rational one!

Discerning the origins of our universe and of mankind boils down to answering four fundamental questions, "How? When? Who? and Why?". Two of these questions fall under the realm of science. These are the questions of "When? and "How?", because science is best equipped to address things that have matter or are measurable. Religion is best equipped to address the questions of "Who? and Why?". Religious based notions or answers can be backed by historical and scientific evidence, as well as rational thought or logic but in the end will require "faith" to accept the resulting notion, answer or dogmatic position. I would argue philosophy is the bridge that helps connect science and faith.

Scientists have now concluded that our world did in fact have a beginning, that it did not just always exist. The scientific community did not always believe or agree on this. It was not until a Catholic priest and scientist, Fr. Georges Lemaître's, "Big Bang Theory" which helped solve a problem Einstein had with his Theory of General Relativity, that scientists have come to accept that our universe had a beginning…and that it will come to an end. I will not go into the details but do check out Fr. Spitzer's Credible Catholic modules for details.

Scientists now agree our universe is roughly fourteen billion years old plus or minus about ten percent. They also believe it started with a "Big Bang", but they cannot tell us who or what caused this bang, what banged, who made whatever banged, nor how man came to be because of this bang. Many scientists believe man evolved along with other plant and animal life forms and that this evolutionary process was a follow-on outcome of the Big Bang. Catholic dogma is not in conflict with the Big Bang Theory or many aspects of evolutionary theory, at least up to the point this theory extends to include "random" events. God's beautifully complex plan of creation was not at all random. However, the Catholic Church strongly believes God was that source, that there was a real purpose, a real plan, a design and order to the whole of creation of our universe and of mankind. And, Jesus is the Son of that God.

There is significant scientific evidence that supports many Christian, as well as many uniquely Catholic dogmatic positions. These include: the existence of our souls (the transcendental, immortal or "God-like" characteristic unique to humans); that a supreme being or God, created our universe; that Jesus was real, was who he said he was, and even that he had an AB blood type; that miracles have happened; and, there is even scientific evidence that suggests this Jesus rose from the dead and ascended into heaven (from scientific studies on the "Shroud of Turin"). Do all scientists agree on all these points? No! Can all these be one hundred percent proven scientifically or in a court of law? Again no (but I like my chances of securing a positive verdict from a "jury of my peers" for the case that could be made")! In the end, belief in God and that Jesus was the Son of God, while having strong scientific, as well as philosophical backing, boils down to a matter of faith.

Before I get to the "gift of faith", let me give you a few thoughts on the philosophical evidence for God as the source of the creation of our universe. As I said, I see philosophy as the bridge between science and faith. The word "philosophy" comes from the Greek words "philo" which means love and "sophia" which means, wisdom.

Again, volumes have been written on the philosophical arguments for a supreme being or a "God" as the creator or cause of our universe and of mankind. Aristotle and other great philosophers "reasoned" there must be a supreme being...and this solves a problem or provides an answer to a question that scientists cannot properly answer. Scientists all agree matter cannot be created or destroyed. They all agree matter can only be modified through natural or human means. Until the Big Bang Theory, they simply believed the universe just "always was" or that it was the result of some very ridiculously low probability, "random event". Even if it could have happened randomly, they could not explain the origin of the "things" or "matters" that had to pre-exist for this highly improbable random event to actually occur. Aristotle and other philosophers' reason that everything has a cause. Your and my "cause" was our parents, and their cause was their parents, etc. But there is general agreement that "matter" cannot be created by natural means, that our universe and mankind had to have a cause that was not bound by natural laws and the limits of time, space or matter. That is, there had to be an "uncaused, first cause", or a supreme being that always was, always will be and is everywhere, all at the same time.

Further reasoning leads to the understanding that there cannot be two supreme beings, there could only be one, as both could not be everywhere at the same time, in the same place, for then they would be in conflict with each other. So, there must be only one supreme being. I know this begs many questions as I just reduced volumes of philosophical arguments down to a few lines of text. Now I will just say either "trust me" or start reading the volumes of material on the philosophical and scientific evidence for God, or a supreme being and come to your own conclusion (Again, I would point you to Fr. Robert J. Spitzer's, Magis Center, specifically the Credible Catholic modules for more details…he provides his own "blue" books of supporting detail for the information presented in these modules). So, let's get back to the question of "faith".

First faith is a gift, a personal one. It starts as a small seed that hopefully you continually and frequently fertilize, water and feed with thought, prayer, reading, education, and for us Catholics, by taking full advantage of all the sacraments and the wealth of resources open to us via the Church. Most of us build on the same seed of faith our parents were blessed with, especially if both parents were of the same faith. Hopefully, as we grow and mature in our education and ability to reason, we ask questions about why we believe what we believe and why particular denominations of faith believe what they believe and then seek out solid answers. I have already stated the Catholic Church believes they are the one true Church or faith, but they also hold that you need not be a baptized Catholic to get to heaven.

While there is a best path, there is more than one path to heaven (strict Evangelicals will disagree with me here). So, for me at least, it starts with first learning more about the faith you were raised in and living a good, strong moral life living the "Great Commandment" to the fullest of your ability. Once you have solidified your faith foundation you can branch out and delve into an examination of other faith denominations to identify and evaluate the similarities and differences between their beliefs and ours as Catholics.

I cannot logically conclude that our unbelievably complex and beautiful universe could have come about in any other way than through the instigation or, creation by a Supreme Being, by God, as part of a well-designed plan. So, it all flows from here. So, after you buy-in to the existence of God and that this God is responsible for creation (I won't argue the degree to which God created versus simply started an evolutionary process) this is the point where various religions begin to differ. All Christians believe that Jesus Christ was and is the Son of God while other non-Christian religions go in various other directions in their belief and definition of who God is. Then, there are thousands of different Christian faith denominations, principally as a result of the Reformation, that differ in specific articles of faith from each other and from Catholic Church beliefs.

I can't go into it here, but at some point, in your faith journey, you should read C.S. Lewis's, Mere Christianity. In this great book Lewis makes a series of layered, rational arguments supporting Christianity's claim that Jesus was and is, who he claimed to be, that is, the Son of God. However, Lewis does not try to make a case for or attempt to convert the reader to any one particular Christian faith denomination. I personally do not think it is healthy for Christians of differing beliefs to spend much "bandwidth" attempting to convert fellow Christians from one Christian denomination to another. While I strongly believe the Catholic Church is the one true Church, I prefer to spend my time and energy: converting atheists to a belief in God; to helping agnostics come to accept the Catholic notion of who God is; to bringing the Good News of Jesus Christ to non-Christians; and, to drawing fallen away Christians/Catholics from their faith in Jesus and from the practice of their faith, back into relationship with Jesus Christ.

As I said, I firmly believe the Catholic Church, is the one true Church and is the best path for me to follow to achieve eternal salvation. However, I strengthened my belief in this path by asking many questions about what Catholics believe and then by asking and seeking out solid answers as to why the Catholic Church holds the dogmatic positions that it does from trusted, authoritative Catholic Church sources. While I may not have liked all the answers or not always "bought in" or fully comprehended the logic (for many faith decisions are not fully explained via logic but do have an underlying logic or rationale), I generally came away feeling stronger that this path was indeed the correct one, the best one. I also looked at the fact that Catholicism is deeply rooted in scripture, is based on a long, rich, and consistent tradition of core beliefs and is based on Jesus as being the Son of God. After reading about Jesus, I eventually determined he either had to be who he said he was, or he had to be the greatest con artist of all times, or he was a complete lunatic? Under scrutiny, only the first conclusion held-up...but I did paraphrase C.S. Lewis's conclusion in Mere Christianity with this point.

So, I pray you can find the answers to your understanding of who God is and to your specific faith questions and that this will set you firmly in the center of the Catholic Church's path to salvation. Regardless, you should know why you practice whatever faith you subscribe to and that you use the gifts, talents and resources you were blessed with as though they are on loan to you and not really yours, certainly not for your own exclusive use and benefit. For they are not "ours", they are gifts that you can and should use to help others and for the greater honor and glory of the God that lent them to you.

2. Does God commonly visit people today (in a visible way)?

God continues to reveal himself to us in many ways but mostly through those we meet every day! Remember each one of us is created in God's image and likeness. Therefore, we as Catholics believe God is present in each one of us regardless of race, color or religion. We believe therefore in the sanctity of life, in the unborn fetus, in the mentally disabled, and in our most senior of citizens. However, much like with St. Thomas, God challenges us to believe without seeing.

I do not have any personal experience, nor do I personally know others who have reported to have seen an image of God. However, there are many events in many saint's lives of miracles, apparitions, healings and other events that defy human or scientific explanation that have been well vetted and attested to as authentic by the Catholic Church.

While God may not be physically present here as the man Jesus, or in some other visible way, he is here with us and works both directly and indirectly through each one of us. Ask nurses and doctors who work in hospitals if they do not often see sick people recover that medically had been given no possible chance for recovery. Look at all the very good deeds and kind acts performed every day. Read the life of Mother Theresa. Several other saints were more recently canonized including: Blessed Mother Theodore Guerin from Terre Haute, IN; Pope John XXIII; Pope John Paul II; and, Pope Paul VI. In fact, our current Pope Francis has already canonized 898 persons as saints in his current Pontificate.

Jesus works through us, through you and me. Jesus's miracles are all around us and performed everyday by him through answered prayers, gifts bestowed on us and by him acting through others. Unfortunately, bad news sells better on TV and rarely do our news programs focus on all the very good and positive things that happen daily in our world.

Remember what Jesus said to Thomas after he appeared to the disciples a second time. Thomas was not there the first time Jesus appeared to his disciples after he rose from the dead. Thomas could not believe and would not accept that Jesus rose from the dead until he could see and touch Jesus. Jesus said to Thomas, on his second visit, when Thomas was present, "Happy are those, who do not see, yet believe". He was not just talking to Thomas, he was also talking directly to you, to me, and to all of those who have yet to come.

We must remember God is always with us. He is all around you, with you, and for you. All we must do is "knock" and the door will be opened. Sometimes he may be slower getting to the door than we would like, and he may choose to answer your knock differently than you would like. He left us seven sacraments, especially the Holy Eucharist where he is with us in the most intimate way possible. He taught us how to pray, and he promised us he would always be with us. We need to pray, to develop a close working relationship with him by always talking to him and by learning more about our faith. We receive grace (help) through prayer, through active participation in mass and through the other sacraments that are open to us.

Our challenge is to understand God's will or plan for us, or for others whom we love, and for whom we may be praying, may be different than our wills, wants and expectations. Also, his timetable for answering prayers may be very different than ours. Some believe God is not listening or responding because he is not giving us what WE want, when WE want it. Au' contraire (thought I would throw some French in since all we have used is Aramaic and Greek in class, but I do not know French, so this may be off a bit??), he is listening and does respond. We may be the ones that are not hearing or responding.

Friendships take work, sacrifice, dialog and love. It is no different in our relationship with God. He made the ultimate sacrifice and shows us his love by being such a forgiving God. We need to hold up our end of the dialog and constantly seek out his help!

Read Matthew Pinto's answer to a related question (#125) in his book, *Did Adam & Eve Have Belly Buttons?* regarding modern day miracles. Pinto points out that examples of modern-day miracles or of God revealing himself to us are too numerous to count. There have been numerous, non-medically explicable miracles of healing. Bodies of dead saints have been found to be incorrupt hundreds of years after their deaths. These can still be seen today (for more information on such miracles, see the powerful books, *Eucharist Miracles* and *The Incorruptibles,* both published by TAN Books).

We also have the Eucharistic miracle in which a consecrated host (which Catholics believe to be transubstantiated into the body of Christ... (formerly plain bread) turned into a visible fleshy bloody tissue. I encourage you to check out information on the scientific studies that were done on this consecrated host that had been accidentally dropped but was recovered by the priest in the church where it was found in Buenos Aires, Argentina. This consecrated host turned into a piece of bloody tissue, that when tested, was found to be a fragment of a heart muscle found in the left ventricle close to the valves and had an AB blood type. This was from the Church of Sanata Maria Y Calballito Almagro and the incident was reported to the local Archbishop Bergoglio (who would later become Pope Francis). For details on this miracle, go to Fr. Robert Spitzer's *Credible Catholic, Why Be Catholic?* module (slides 63-71).

Another well-known miracle we can still see today is that of the tilma (or cloak) St. Juan Diego was wearing when he saw the apparition of Our Lady in Guadalupe, Mexico. It bears a miraculous image of Our Lady. The tilma itself should have disintegrated years ago since it is over four hundred years old, yet it still shows little sign of age. Science cannot explain any of these things. Details on the tilma can also be found in Fr. Robert Spitzer's, *Credible Catholic* modules, specifically the module entitled, *Why Be Catholic?* (slides 45-55).

Lastly, for yet another miracle science has been able to provide supportive evidence, that Jesus rose from the dead and resurrected, you need to read about the "Shroud of Turin" and the scientific testing that was done on this cloth which is believed to contain the image of the resurrected Jesus. The testing revealed that the image on the shroud required a burst of energy and light more powerful than the technology of that time could ever have generated. For details on this miracle and the evidence to support it, go on-line to Fr. Robert Spitzer's *Credible Catholic* modules, specifically the one entitled, *Proof of Jesus' Resurrection and Divinity,* (slides 25-56).

However, despite all the "scientific evidence" for the above referenced miracles, it still requires faith to fully embrace them. I truly believe God reveals himself through those we encounter every single day. We must keep Jesus's message to St. Thomas in mind, "happy are those who do not see, yet believe". While God may not ever directly appear to you or me, or anyone that we may personally know, we can see God's image in our classmates, in our friends, in those we see in the mall, in ball parks, in offices and everywhere we go. We simply must use our eyes to see and our ears to hear God in all whom we encounter. Jesus's message to us was that if we truly opened are hearts, ears, minds, and whole beings to his gospel messages, we would be transformed. We have seen many examples of people totally turning their lives' around once they had an opportunity to hear and listen to His "Good News" as revealed in Sacred Scripture.

There is a famous former Chicago Tribune writer named Lee Strobel who was an atheist. Not only did he not believe there was a God, he certainly did not believe Jesus Christ was the Son of God, one person in the Trinity. However, Mr. Strobel decided to investigate who this person called Jesus really was. He retired from the Tribune and spent a very long time researching and interviewing respected people from various faiths with strong scriptural, cultural, historical and linguistic backgrounds. He talked to those that believed in Jesus and those that did not. He researched what was written about Jesus from a variety of secular and non-secular sources. He admits that while he tried to approach his research like a reporter, objectively and by putting his personal biases behind, he still went into the project biased against believing that Jesus was anything more than an influential person.

He ultimately came to believe that Jesus was real and that he was who he claimed to be, the Son of God. Through this process he converted from atheism to Christianity. He captures this whole story in his book *The Case for the Real Jesus.* I encourage you to read this book when you are in high school or college or older. This is an excellent example of God revealing himself to Lee Strobel and to us in our modern-day world even though God never appeared directly before Mr. Strobel.

3. If some parts of the Bible were verbally passed down from generation to generation and other parts are stories, aren't they going to be changed little by little each time they are passed down? How can we know today's Bible is credible?

You make two good points. One is that a portion of the Bible has stories or parables in it (mostly in the New Testament) and the other is that much of the Bible was handed down verbally from one generation to the next (mostly the Old Testament) before it was written down. This is known as the "oral tradition".

Let me take your last point first. You are correct! Many of the details in the verbal multi-generational transmission of biblical accounts probably did change by accident or even design during the telling and re-telling. However, one should not equate this oral tradition from an accuracy point of view, with today's "telephone game" as some critics of biblical Christianity have done. The oral tradition of handing down scripture was taken extremely seriously by the early Jewish people. This oral tradition is nowhere near the equivalent of your parents telling and re-telling certain bedtime stories.

If I told a fictional (made-up) story in a historically accurate setting, would it make the historically accurate part any less believable? Conversely, if I told a true (non-fictional) story about an event in my life but changed some of the names or places referenced or some irrelevant facts to protect the privacy of myself or others in the story, would that make my story any less true or believable? Would the message I intended be any less accurate, authentic or credible?

My grandchildren love me to tell them bedtime stories about when I was a little boy. Some of these stories are one hundred percent true, others are made up to convey a message or moral value. These started out as mere entertainment but as I retold the stories over and over, my older grandchildren would quickly correct me if I changed any key details or left anything out. The Jewish people took the oral tradition of these scriptural stories much more seriously. They were not told for entertainment value but as important truths and messages that were to be passed on or taught to their children and then to their children's children, etc.

The Bible is not intended to be a historically factual account, but it is intended to be one hundred percent accurate in terms of conveying the message God intended us to hear and understand. Bishop Robert Barron reminds us that the Bible is more like a library than a book, it has a mix of literary styles, reflective of the various times, intentions, backgrounds, knowledge, etc. of the various authors that contributed to the Bible as we Catholics know it (remember the Jewish Bible differs from the Catholic Bible and the Catholic Bible differs from other Christian versions in terms of the content included, or purposely excluded, but I will not go into these differences here). For example, many of the books are poetic while others are filled with parables, stories to convey a message (like some of my stories to my grandchildren) and were never intended to be taken literally or factually.

Catholics and many Christian faiths believe the following three things about the Bible:

1. It is an inspired work. That is, it was inspired by God but written by men in the words of men. These men included and excluded events, acts or teachings as God inspired them and they all wrote within the limits of their abilities and knowledge.
2. It is an infallible work. The Bible is infallible in terms of telling me the truth when it comes to matters of faith and practice. It is one hundred percent accurate in terms of delivering the message God intended.

3.   It is inerrant. The Bible is inerrant in terms of what it "teaches" but this does not mean it is intended to be one hundred percent historical or factual in how that message is taught or delivered.

So yes, many books of the Bible were not intended to be one hundred percent factual or to be historical realities, but the intended message is fully accurate and without error. This is important to remember when we now cover your concerns about the believability of the "stories" in the Bible. If your issue is whether you should believe all the details or "facts" or if the stories are one hundred percent historically accurate, no you should not believe this. The Catholic Church does not teach this and in some cases even the original biblical authors may not have been sure of all the facts or meant those parts to be "factual". Remember, I explained the number forty is used in the Bible quite often. Many biblical scholars believed that using the number forty was used intentionally to imply a "relatively" long time (depending on whether they were referencing days, weeks, years, etc.) but used this number when they were not sure just how long the time-period actually was.

Some whole books of the Bible are poetic in style such as Genesis and Psalms. The key in poetic books, even more so then in other books of the Bible, is to focus on the message not the "facts" or details. As I mentioned earlier, Genesis has two accounts of creation. The point of the messages delivered in the Book of Genesis is that God created or caused man (and women) to be created and men ultimately sinned against God requiring God to sacrifice his Son to free us from the pain and suffering of our sins. In the parable of "*The Good Samaritan*", we hear of a man who gets beaten and robbed and several ignore the beaten man but then a hated Samaritan takes pity on him. The message was that all men are our "brothers" and those that are more fortunate have an obligation to help those less fortunate. This was a story Jesus told to deliver his intended message.

The Bible is not in conflict with science. In fact, science and faith work in concert with each other so long as each stay within its respective areas of strength. For example, regarding the origins of our universe or of man, both science and faith, or the Bible have their place, their areas of "fit".

Science and faith work most effectively together when science focuses on the questions of "when" and "how", while faith or the Bible focus on the questions of "who" and "why". It is important for us to focus on the meaning or intended message of the Bible, not on the literary styles or historical accuracy of the details used in the Bible.

4. In the Book of Job, why did Jesus have to prove himself to Satan? And, if God is all powerful, all knowing and all loving, why does he allow evil and suffering in our world?

The Book of Job is a one of my favorite books in the Old Testament. You should know this book is a poetic, didactic book, not necessarily a historical one. That means this book was written to teach, to deliver a specific message to us not to convey historical facts. Biblical scholars are not even sure who the author of this book was but believe it was written between the 7th and 5th centuries B.C.

Satan, as referenced in this book is technically not the devil but a title for adversary. So, remember the Book of Job is a story intended to deliver a message. The message is all about how to deal with adversity in our lives and that we need to accept both the good things we are given along with the problems, even very hard ones, as blessings from God. God is giving us these blessings and allowing the bad things to happen as part of his overall redemptive plan. Good and bad things happen to good and bad people ubiquitously.

Just because he knows ahead of time what decisions we will make; they are no less "our" decisions. Our lives are pre-known by God but not predetermined by God. If I could travel in time and see who would win this year's Super Bowl and then return to the present time, my knowledge of who would win would in no way affect all the individual decisions the coaches and players will ultimately make on what plays to run and how to run them and thus who eventually wins the game. So, our lives our not predetermined, predestined or out of our control just because God knows in advance what we decisions we will make.

God knew we would not always use this gift wisely. Just like he created Lucifer, and the other angels who rebelled against God and were ultimately forced out of heaven by St. Michael, God does not control how we use the gifts he gave us. He knew we would make bad decisions and that there would have to be consequences for these bad decisions. Evil would temporarily triumph. Randy Alcorn reminds us in his book "If God is Good", that God did not create evil, nor does he cause evil, but he does permit evil to exist and he uses evil things and evil people for his ultimate purpose. Some of the consequences of evil or bad decisions are pain, suffering and death. However, God paid the ultimate sacrifice for all our bad or evil ways by sacrificing his only begotten (not made) son to overcome sin and death. This was part of his plan of "redemptive salvation".

Like Job from the Old Testament, or others you may know, like my good friend Jim Harrell who died of the terrible disease of ALS, God calls many of us to carry an extra burden by asking us to accept challenges in our lives', so we too can participate in His overall plan of redemptive salvation. Like other choices we are enabled to make, we can either accept these challenges willingly and gracefully and use them as gifts to help others and give honor and glory to God, or we can turn bitter and cry, "why me God"?

Back in the Old Testament times, people did not understand this (such as Job's own wife and three friends). They felt anyone who was afflicted with a disease or a handicap, a physical impairment of some kind, that this was given to them as a direct consequence for their own personal sin or that of their parents. They did not understand God's real plan. Pain and suffering are consequences for the general sinful nature of man. And, while God asks some to carry more than their fair share of the pain, he does so with a plan and a purpose. Often, he provides extra blessings of faith, grace and inner strength to help them deal with the burden they have been asked to carry.

And all his creations were "good". But then there was "The Fall" when man, tempted by the "evil one" exercised free will and sinned against God causing a separation of "man" from "God". The power of sin and suffering enters the world.

But, as you rightly pointed out in your question, God is all powerful. He could have immediately corrected or stopped this evil right then, but he loved us too much to override our free will. He wanted to give each one of us the opportunity to choose him freely, not be forced into a relationship with him. Had he done this, instead of being persons created uniquely in his own image and likeness with free wills to choose right over wrong, we would have become the equivalent of robots or lesser forms of his own creation! God is all loving, but he does not force himself on us.

In fact, he is so loving he sent his only begotten Son, who became incarnate, dwelt among us, taught us by his own example, and then let us torture and crucify him. But he overcame sin and death by rising from the dead and ascending into heaven and he left us a Church and blessed us with the Holy Spirit and his seven gifts and twelve fruits to help us on our journey. While it is given that Jesus, the Son-of-God, paid the ultimate price for our brokenness; and that we cannot "earn" our way into heaven; we do have to exercise our free wills by intentionally "choosing" him, every day, through our thoughts, words and actions. And yet, when we do reject him, through choosing evil over good, he is an all merciful, all forgiving God as we repent, atone and re-commit to amend our sinful ways.

Deacon Keith Strohm, from the Archdiocese of Chicago, in a recent discipleship formation session offered the following insights into this question of why God permits suffering and evil. Deacon Keith explains:

"God is not the author of suffering, he does not directly or intentionally send suffering" (Mt 7:11, Lk 11:11). Suffering, illness and death are all linked to the fall, which the Father has definitively dealt in and through his son Jesus Christ.

Because of the life, death, resurrection, and ascension of Jesus Christ, the reality of suffering has been transformed. Suffering now has meaning and potential "fruit". Every experience of suffering becomes now an opportunity for openness, repentance, grace, healing, transformation, and, ultimately, salvation for us and others. Although God chose not to override free will and instantly reverse the effects of the Fall, in Jesus the Father uses the brokenness of this world for our own good, perfection, and salvation when we remain united with him.

Ultimately, it is ALWAYS God's will to heal, otherwise he would never have sent Jesus to us or bestow grace through the Sacrament. If we remain with him, our healing will be completely finished at the "Second Coming", the Lord can bring healing to us within the context of our lives. We can directly and deliberately seek healing—both natural and supernatural. We are reminded that Jesus healed as a sign of the Father's power over sin (Lk 5:17-26); as confirmation of his message to us; and, as proof of his true identity. As the content of the message made manifest: healing is synonymous with the breaking through of "God's Kingdom."

Often people need to be healed and delivered so they can freely respond to the Father's invitation to salvation in Jesus Christ! Because the human person is an "embodied spirit" there is an integrity between body, mind, and spirit. The paschal dimension of Christ's life is intended to set the whole human person free not just one aspect. Thus, Jesus's ministry of healing was central to his messianic mission, he came to save, deliver, heal, preserve, protect, and make whole.

"Jesus" means, according to Hebrew, "Savior," but in the Greek tongue it means "healer"; since he is physician of souls and bodies, curer of spirits, curing the blind in body, and leading minds into light, healing the visibly lame, and guiding sinners' steps to repentance, saying to the crippled, "Sin no more, and, take up your bed and walk."

Jesus's entire mission was one of restoration, liberation, deliverance, renewal, and healing—salvation. He gathered the Church, starting with the first disciples, empowered them, and then sent them out to complete his work of salvation to all the earth. The ministry of healing was (and is) central to Jesus's proclamation of the Kingdom. Through ministry and sacramental life through the work of lay apostles sent into the world to make the Kingdom present in word and deed—especially through the charisms provided by the Holy Spirit to each of us at Baptism. He said to them,

> "Go into the whole world and proclaim the gospel to every creature. Whoever believes and is baptized will be saved; whoever does not believe will be condemned. These signs will accompany those who believe: in my name they will drive out demons, they will speak new languages. They will pick up serpents [with their hands], and if they drink any deadly thing, it will not harm them. They will lay hands on the sick, and they will recover" (Mk 16:15-18).

So, the supernatural work of healing is accomplished through Christians who possess some or all of the following: baptismal authority in Jesus through the Holy Spirit; particular authority through Holy Orders; Charisms (in particular the charism of healing); or a particular ministry of healing and deliverance."

So, our God is indeed a "Loving Father" who would not inflict pain and suffering on us …just to make us better or stronger, what father would do that? God is indeed and all loving, all merciful and all forgiving Father who wants to heal our brokenness of mind, body, spirit and soul!

This is what the Book of Job is all about. Not all respond well and accept the burden and the graces for what they are. These challenges present opportunities to both save ourselves and to help others achieve salvation by the example we can set and by willingly accepting these challenges and using them for God's greater honor and glory.

5. If medical experts have not revealed a body part, the soul, how do you know it exists?

No doctor or scientist will ever find a body part that can be identified as the soul. Our soul is a spiritual, free and immortal aspect of our humanness individually created by God and infused into the human body at conception

(Fr. John S. Hardon, *The Catholic Question and Answer Catechism*). Our soul is our spiritual essence given to us by God, while our parents give us our human essence, and both occur at the time we are conceived in our mother's womb. Since the soul is not something we can touch or feel, we cannot scientifically prove it exists.

However, we can listen to God's inspired scriptural teachings and apply our ability to reason to "get comfortable" with the understanding that we have a soul. It is your very soul that gives you the ability to question its existence. It is our soul that separates us from other life forms. No other animal or plant can reason, exercise a free will, has a conscience, etc. We can also "know" we have a soul by reading the Bible (Genesis Chapter 1, or Wisdom 3:1-4). Lastly, the Pope and the Magisterium of the church have proclaimed the existence of our souls and their immortal quality. Our bodies will turn to dust when we die but it is our souls that live forever. Makes sense doesn't it?

The soul is the part of our individuality that came from an immortal, supreme, spiritual being. Our souls are our only immortal and spiritual quality. It is how we live our lives on earth that determines the eternal home for our immortal spiritual essence known as our souls. On the final judgment day our souls will be re-united with our now glorified bodies. I encourage you to go on-line to www.crediblecatholic.com and look at module one, *Medical Evidence and Philosophical Proof of a Soul* from The Magis Center's, *The Credible Catholic* series of seven modules. This module provides scientific "evidence" which supports...but cannot not fully prove the existence of souls. This full series addresses many myths about science and faith. In this module, results from numerous scientific studies of people who suffered clinical death (brain stops functioning) and were subsequently revived, but who also reported having "Near Death Experiences" or NDEs, were reviewed. The studies cited were only credible ones that were scientifically and objectively substantiated by reliable doctors and other hospital authorities and where the experiences reported by patients could be vetted and validated. The module focuses on five of many other studies that repeatedly confirmed that clinically dead patients were able to hear and see things despite being clinically dead. These abilities and experiences help validate that we have souls or a consciousness that are not dependent upon our bodies or our brains which allows us to responsibly conclude that we do in fact have souls. These souls can and do transcend our normal mortal lives consistent with Church teaching.

6. Is there any scientifically verifiable data to support what we uniquely believe as Catholics or does it all boil down to having to take a huge "blind leap of faith" to believe all these teachings?

There most certainly is a significant amount of scientific evidence to "support" many aspects of core Catholic dogmatic positions and Church teachings. I wish I had the time, space and knowledge to talk you through all of them! In this space I will set the foundation and encourage you to dig deeper into the wealth of evidence that does support these positions.

If you remember, I asked on the first day of class if any of you had a parent or close family relative who was a lawyer. I explained that we were going to focus on many of the very uniquely Catholic teachings or dogmas and that I was going to give you all the reasons or evidence I could to support belief in these positions. I told you that I very much liked my chances in a court of law with the evidence I could present. In many court cases, the final decision comes down to what a legal standard known as a "preponderance of the evidence". Another higher or tougher legal standard is "beyond a reasonable doubt". There is a real difference between these two legal standards. The first, "the preponderance of the evidence" standard is used in civil cases and requires that at least fifty-one percent of the evidence shown, favors the plaintiff's position and outcome. Another way to think of the standard is to simply ask whether the plaintiff's proposition is more likely to be true than not true. If the judge or jury concludes that the evidence suggests that the plaintiff's argument is more likely to be true or accurate, the decision goes the plaintiff's way.

However, the higher legal standard is "beyond a reasonable doubt". Legal scholars generally describe the "beyond a reasonable doubt" standard as being met when the prosecutor demonstrates that there is no plausible reason to believe otherwise. If there is any real doubt after careful consideration of all the evidence presented, then this standard has not been met. However, this does not mean that the "beyond a reasonable doubt" standard is absolute, the prosecutor must prove the case to an extent that no reasonable person could reasonably doubt the defendant's guilt or disagree with the prosecutor's position.

I told you I believed a "doctor of the Church" or a scholar of Catholic Church teaching (I did not count myself as one of these lofty personages) could easily meet the preponderance of the evidence standard and in most but not all cases of key Catholic dogmatic positions could meet the even higher "beyond a reasonable doubt" standard. I admitted achieving this higher "beyond a reasonable doubt" standard would be more difficult. I hope that as I presented the evidence for these positions, I at least met the standard of "preponderance of the evidence" and that you came away believing these articles of faith, these dogmatic positions, the Catholic Church teachings we had time to cover were in fact credible, believable and likely true. Whether or not I achieved the higher "beyond a reasonable doubt" standard, I do not know. However, as you may recall I reminded you that while there is much scientific, philosophical and rational evidence for these positions, in the end it will boil down to faith. However, this need not and should not be a "blind" leap of faith but rather a very rational, well thought out, logical "faith based" leap or conclusion or set of conclusions.

As one progresses through the list of Catholic faith-based positions, some are easier to "defend" or create a winning "beyond a reasonable doubt" based decision. For example, it is much easier to "prove" there is one God who is the creator of us and our universe, than it is to defend the doctrine of the Trinity, that is, there being three persons in one God...and yet all Christians and Catholics alike accept this doctrine. It is easier to defend that Jesus is who he claimed to be, the Son of God, than it is to defend that Mary was assumed body and soul into heaven shortly after her death.

There is scientific evidence to help support that Jesus rose from the dead (read about the Shroud of Turin) and that Jesus and his appointed successors can change bread and water into God's body and blood (read about the scientific tests done on a consecrated host that had been dropped on the floor of a church in Argentina, that ultimately turned into bloody tissue which tested to be AB+ blood type from a human heart) but these dogmatic positions still require faith. I strongly encourage you to go through Fr. Robert J. Spitzer's Magis Center seven *Credible Catholic* modules that focus on these very topics and many others. They provide significant scientific and rational evidence for many of the Catholic Church's dogmatic positions. They also de-bunk the false myth that science and faith conflict with each other.

I encourage you to read what is readily available such as: the lives' of the saints; the Church's rigorous process for declaring persons as saints, documented appearances of the Blessed Mother to hundreds and in one case thousands of people, of verified Near Death Experiences during clinical death (that support the Catholic doctrine that we have immortal souls), of countless other miraculous healings that the medical community cannot explain, and of course, read Sacred Scripture. As compelling as these materials may be and other available evidentiary materials, much will still require a rational faith-based component to fully accept as true.

7. Why is Jesus (God) only present when two or more are meeting (gathered) in his name? Why not when just one person is praying?

You are referring to Matthew's Gospel, when he reminds us of Jesus's promise when he said, "whenever two or more are gathered in my name (in prayer), I am there in your midst" (Mt 18:20). While Jesus's basic message is for us to gather collectively in prayer, for there is strength and comfort in numbers, there is more to the story. Often, when I go to bed at night, I am very tired and sometimes don't feel like praying. But then my wife will ask me if I am ready to pray. I know there are many nights I don't pray because by myself I am weak. I also know there are many more nights that I do pray because my wife is there with me and for me. We can have the same impact on others. I started saying the Rosary after the 8:00 AM mass during the week because others were already praying it. Their presence gave me the impetus to stay a bit longer and pray the Rosary and to pray with them. We pray for common intentions and for personal ones. Jesus assures us he is present and hearing our prayers when we are gathered collectively.

However, this does not mean God isn't also present when only one is praying? He does not say I am ONLY present when two or more are gathered....!

You also need to know a little about Matthew and one of the key themes that is more unique to Matthew's Gospel. Matthew is primarily writing to the Jewish community and relates Jesus's life, his teachings, and his purposes, in a way that will resonate with the Jewish community. Matthew suggests that Jesus personifies Torah and then makes the case to declare Jesus is "Torah made human". Torah was and is very important to the Jewish people and to their religious tradition. Matthew includes this saying from Jesus to tie Jesus's teachings to the Torah. Matthew uses symbolic associations of Torah in connection with Jesus throughout his entire gospel. In the Torah there is a similar reference to prayer Matthew uses in verse 18:20. This saying is like one attributed to a rabbi executed in 135 A.D. at the time of the second Jewish revolt.... "when two sit and there are between them the words of the Torah, the divine presence (Shekinah) rests upon them."

I believe what you are asking is, what was the meaning, or what is the message behind this famous scriptural quote? Is God dissing anyone who prays by themselves? Not at all! He is delivering a positive message of what can happen when two or more come together to pray. He is not saying the same benefits will not be afforded to those who independently pray. You also need to read the context in which Jesus makes this statement as reported in Matthew's gospel. Jesus has just given Peter as the first pope, the power to forgive sin. He also has just reminded us that to get to heaven we must be like little children, innocent and pure. Even more forcefully, he promises that it would be better for anyone of us to tie a stone around our neck and jump in the sea (drown ourselves) rather than lead any of his children astray...into sin by our words or actions). He cautions us to pray so we do not weaken and give-in to the devil's temptations. We need much help if we are to be successful in defeating the devil. One of the devil's many tactics is to is to isolate us, to divide and conquer. He knows that alone we are more vulnerable to his temptations and to succumbing to dark thoughts he can put in our heads. Jesus knows these devilish tactics and teaches us to pray together, to stay together, to help one another and to pray for each other.

In fact, by researching this concept further I found at least five different messages Jesus was delivering through this passage. There is some overlap in these five different messages but each one has a unique point or aspect.

1. Jesus was reminding us of our obligation but also of the benefit of observing the Second Commandment, keeping Holy the Sabbath, i.e. going to mass, at least every Sunday (or Saturday night). The benefit is He will be there with us and for us. So independent of independent prayer, for there is no actual commandment that we must pray, but there is one to go to mass (yes, the assumption is that you pray when you are there), Jesus is saying if you want me to be with you, come to me at mass and receive me in the Holy Eucharist. I will be there for you. Going to mass, by default, requires a minimum of two people to be present.
2. Jesus is encouraging us to pray and to pray together. There is strength in numbers, and we are encouraged by others presence in communal prayer and we help strengthen others by being there with them and for them. We build up added grace and strength to resist the devil's attempts to lead us into occasions for sin and to actual sinful acts. The more we pray, the more likely we are to be able to resist the devil's powerful attempts. It is easier to stand up to an enemy with others helping you and around you then when you are there all by yourself.
3. Jesus is encouraging family formation and development through prayer. Remember the saying, "the family that prays together stays together"? Much like he is encouraging us to pray as a community, providing and drawing strength from each other, he reminds us of the power of the family unit. He is talking to parents and

to children, encouraging to develop a regular practice of family prayer.

4. He is encouraging us to pray for others, to be good Christians. He knows when we come together in prayer, the fact that we are praying as a group will lead to us praying not just for ourselves and for what we want, but to pray for others, especially for those who may not be strong enough to pray for themselves. Think of those who have not been blessed to come from a strong family or from a positive community and have joined gangs, reverted to a life of crime, drugs or other temptation. These people need our prayers.

5. He is reminding us that church is community and that we have an obligation to help all members of our community. He is saying we should pray as a community and that the mass is the ideal setting for such communal prayer. Therefore, when we come to mass, we should not sit there and pray independently (there is a time and a place for this type of prayer), we should join in prayer and song together. So, you see he is telling us not only to pray as a community but how to do so, which circles all the way back to my first point.

The reward for all the above is God will be with us and will help us! Remember Jesus's mother Mary appeared several times to children encouraging them to pray the Holy Rosary together building on the theme of "wherever two or more are gathered, God is present". Mary encourages us to pray the Holy Rosary together as families, as communities…two or more of us, for peace in the world!

8. What happens to people of other non-Christian religious beliefs when they die? Will Muslims, Buddhists and Jews get to heaven?

The same question could be asked regarding members of other faiths, Christian and otherwise, as well as agnostics and atheists. However, neither I nor the Catholic Church believe our salvation is decided by groups or by faith denomination with members of certain faiths being accepted and others not, solely based on the "church" one officially belongs to or fails to belong to. The Catholic Church does not believe that only Catholics can get to heaven. However, you should know that many Christian denominations believe that only "Christians" can get to heaven. They believe you must formally accept Jesus Christ as your "Lord and Savior" to be saved. Many Christians also believe once you formally accept Jesus as your Lord and Savior you will get to heaven, no matter how you live your life here on earth (doctrine of *sola fide,* by faith alone). Catholics, who are also Christians by definition, do not believe this. While being baptized, having a personal relationship with Jesus, and living a good Catholic life in full communion with Jesus is the best path to heaven, it is not the only path.

The Catholic Church is a universal Church and it is open to all. There is no Catholic monopoly on heaven. While the Church does believe Baptism is a critical Sacrament for achieving eternal life in heaven, it need not be a Catholic baptism. Furthermore, the Catholic Church maintains that while Baptism is the ordinary means of achieving salvation, it is not the only means. The "Catechism of the Catholic Church" covers both these points in section 1257:

> The Lord himself affirms that Baptism is necessary for salvation. He also commands his disciples to proclaim the gospel to all nations and to baptize them. Baptism is necessary for salvation for those to whom the gospel has been proclaimed and who have had the possibility of asking for the sacrament. The Church does not know of any means other than Baptism that assures entry into eternal beatitude; this is why she takes care not to neglect the mission she has received from the Lord to see that all who can be baptized are "reborn of water and the spirit." *God has bound salvation to the sacrament of Baptism, but he himself is not bound by the sacraments.*

So, while the sacrament of Baptism is the "ordinary" means, a necessary pre-requisite for salvation, it is not the only means, for God is not limited or bound by the sacraments he gave us.

To be clear, the Catholic Church's infallible position is that there is no salvation apart from Christ and his One, Holy, Catholic, and Apostolic Church. However, the Church maintains that those who never knew Christ or had an opportunity to be in relationship with him will not be held responsible for this lack of knowledge and relationship. Those that truly are ignorant of Christ and his Church still have the real possibility of salvation.

This begs the question, "Who will be saved, and who will not?" Can a Jew, Muslim or a Buddhist get to heaven since as such they never accepted Jesus Christ as God? The Church says yes, they can, even though they may never directly accept the risen Christ Jesus as God, as their Lord and Savior. And yet, I do not feel this is inconsistent with John's Gospel "I am the way the truth and the life, no one comes to the Father except through me" (Jn 14:6). So how can this be possible?

I believe, as Fr. Hardon said, and as our *Catechism of the Catholic Church* confirms, sanctifying grace is available to all men. I believe in a most forgiving God, and in the dimension of God portrayed by the popular Christian author Randy Alcorn, of a patient God who will not stop evil from happening if only to give more time for evil doers to change their ways and turn to him (directly or indirectly). He lets us exercise our own free wills to accept him, to accept his gift of life and gift of grace, even if that decision is to reject the gift.

Fr. Hardon in his book, *The Question and Answer Catholic Catechism,* defines grace as "a supernatural gift that, through the merits of Jesus Christ, God freely bestows on human beings in order to bring them to eternal life. Grace is called a supernatural gift because we have absolutely no right to it, and because its purpose is to lead us to heaven, which is our supernatural destiny." He goes on to say, "divine grace is available to us because Christ died for **all** mankind. All are in fact, called to the same destiny, which is heaven". There are seven pages from this book I would love to share with you if I could (so read his book someday) as they define the two forms of grace, actual and sanctifying, and how they lead to supernatural merit. Fr. Hardon says, "Supernatural merit is that quality of a good act which gives the one who performs it, the right to be rewarded by God, in this life and in the life to come. We can supernaturally merit for ourselves an increase in sanctifying grace and the infused virtues, actual graces and a title to them, the right to enter heaven if we die in the divine friendship and enjoy an increase of happiness in heaven."

I liken it to John 6:22-71, where Jesus tells the people and his disciples that he is the bread of life and that they must eat his body and drink his blood to have eternal life. He meant this literally and reinforced that he meant it literally, even at the expense of losing followers, including some of his own disciples (as he foretold), who found this teaching "too difficult". He did not literally mean that they needed to start gnawing on his arms or legs devouring his flesh and blood to have eternal life (although the literal translation of the Greek word would imply this). He was telling them that he would leave them and us, after rising from the dead, the miracle of transubstantiation, the gift of the Holy Eucharist, so we could literally eat his body and drink his blood. So, his literal directive could be achieved but not via the literal understanding most had when they heard Jesus preach this to them. It is this same literal, but potentially different literal understanding of how John 14:6 might have been meant by Christ.

> The Catholic Church teaches that, Muslims, Buddhists, Jews, et al, those who, through no fault of their own, do not know Christ and his Church: "Those who, through no fault of their own, do not know the Gospel of Christ or his Church, but who nevertheless seek God with a sincere heart, and, moved by grace, try in their actions to do his will as they know it through the dictates of their conscience – those too may achieve eternal salvation" (quoting, Lumen Gentium, 16).

> Many people are raised in non-Christian faiths and never really get the opportunity to "know" Jesus and to accept him as the Son of God, as their Lord and Savior. However, the Catholic Church believes that if these people respond to God's love for them, that is, to the God they have come to know and believe in, with their own love through a personal relationship

and commitment they too will receive sanctifying grace. It is this state of grace through personal response to God's love for us that is the key to eternal salvation.

This helps reaffirm my personal belief that a broad interpretation of John 14:6 is possible without contradicting its literal meaning and there truly is the hope of salvation for non-Christians and non-baptized persons. However, one thing remains clear, belief in Jesus as our savior and living our lives in accordance with that belief, is the best path to eternal life in heaven with God. So, the more people we can lead to Christ, or back to Christ (for those who may have strayed off course), through our words and actions, is exactly what Jesus wants us to do as Christians. The challenge is to use our daily encounters, whether they be with family, schoolmates, social, business or otherwise, to lead others to Jesus. Of course, this must be done in a balanced, inviting, and loving way so as to not turn people off or away, but also not to use fear of coming off weird or strange as an excuse or a rationalization not to speak out at all.

But before I end, what about those who did have an opportunity to know Christ but rejected him? What happens to fallen away Catholics or Christians, can they still get to heaven? Scripture is very clear in this area. "He who hears you hears me, and he who rejects you rejects me" (Luke 10:16). The Church is "the fullness of him who fills all in all" (Eph. 1:23). The Church is Christ in the world. It is almighty God who willed "that through the church the manifold wisdom of God might now be made known" (Ephesians 3:10). To reject the Church is to reject Christ because it was Christ who gave authority to the Church and declared, "If he refuses to listen even to the church, let him be to you as a Gentile or a tax collector. Truly, I say to you, whatever you bind on earth shall be bound in heaven, and whatever you loose on earth shall be loosed in heaven" (Mt 18:17-18).

In short, you cannot separate rejecting the Church with rejecting Christ according to Scripture and the teaching of the Catholic Church. In other words, one cannot just create his own religion and follow the "Jesus" of his own creation and choosing without there being eternal consequences. Anyone who knowingly and deliberately rejects the Church will not achieve eternal salvation. However, it could very well be that a person who left the Church may have had such a distorted notion of what the Church truly is and what she teaches that they might not be held accountable or could still achieve eternal salvation. There may not be culpability. We simply do not know; this will be up to God.

In summary:

- Catholics do not have a monopoly on heaven. And just because we believe, or we accept Jesus as our Lord and Savior and lead good lives, it does not automatically mean we have a free pass to heaven, we must directly respond, return God's love for us back to him. We must live the Great Commandment, just as atheists and people of other faiths must do. We don't earn our way into heaven but as St. James said, "faith without works is dead".

- That said, there can only be one true God and one true Church and the Catholic Church, which is a universal church, excludes no one and believes it is that one true Church (which I agree with) but that does not mean you must be Catholic to get to heaven.

- In the case of one who is truly ignorant of the truth of the Catholic Faith, "through no fault of [his] own," he can be saved via extraordinary means not by just living a good life. That is, he must return the love of his understanding of who God is, in a way that opens his soul to sanctifying grace.

- No one who knowingly and deliberately rejects Christ will be saved. It doesn't matter how good of a fallen away Christian, Muslim, Jew, Baptist, or anything else he may be. If anyone rejects the truth of Christ and his Church—even one definitive teaching—they will be lost. However, a person could have such a distorted notion of Christ or Christianity that they may not be culpable and could still achieve eternal salvation.

- We do not know the extent of God's mercy and forgiveness despite the extent of man's ability, frequency and propensity to sin. We also do not know what was in men's heart's, even the most sinful ones, prior to their death. Remember, Jesus forgave those who crucified him even while they were in the act of doing so. Also, one of the criminals, who, to the best of our knowledge, had never been baptized and admitted that he deserved to be crucified, was forgiven and was promised to be in heaven that very day. God is our sole and final judge. So, we have much reason to be optimistic about our chances of getting to heaven.

9. What makes Catholicism different from any other religious faith denomination?

There are many doctrines, dogmas and beliefs we have in common with most other Christian faiths but that would not be shared by other religions like Islam and Buddhism, etc. All Christians believe Jesus Christ was the Son of God and that he is one of three persons in the Trinity, but that there is one God.

Dogmas that are indigenous to Catholicism include but are not limited to:

a. The Real Presence of Christ in the Eucharist - Catholics believe when the priest consecrates the bread and wine on the altar at mass its substance or essence changes into God's body and blood, it is not just symbolic! Thus, the dogma of transubstantiation.

b. The Infallibility of the Pope when speaking "ex cathedra" or "from the throne" on matters of Catholic dogma (he can still fail a math exam!). - This means the Pope cannot make a mistake in any official dogmatic position. Catholics believe in the Authority of the Church. The magisterium is the teaching authority of the Church which helps guide the Pope and helps us discern the "message God intended" throughout Sacred Scripture and how that message applies to our ever-changing world.

c. The Virgin Birth - Mary giving birth to Jesus without having sexual relations with a man, her husband Joseph.

d. The Immaculate Conception - Mary being born without original sin!

e. The Assumption of Mary Body and Soul into Heaven – That shortly after death, Mary as the New Testament equivalent to the Old Testament Arc of the Covenant, like her Immaculate Conception, consistent with preserving her "perfected" nature, was spared the human decay of her body and assumed both body and soul into heaven where she reigns as Mother of Heaven and Earth.

f.   Praying to Mary and the Communion of Saints – The act of asking Mary and the saints to intercede for us. Catholics are not asking Mary or the saints to directly answer our prayers but are asking them to intercede on our behalf. Regarding the use of sacramentals, we do not pray to, or worship, statues in Church or in Catholic shrines. Catholics use these as "God-pointers" to help them focus when they pray and as reminders to pray! They are not idols or false gods as were so common throughout the Old Testament.

10. What are the teachings about death in the Catholic Church?

Fr. Hardon's, *The Question and Answer Catholic Catechism,* does a great job of clearly addressing questions about death and salvation. Father Hardon would tell you there are twelve articles of faith in the Apostles Creed, your question deals with the seventh article which is, "from thence he shall come to judge the living and the dead". This article teaches there will be a general judgment at the end of times, at the end of the world, which will determine whether we will go to heaven or hell based on the "moral good or evil each of us has done". This last phrase would require pages to explain so I will refrain from trying to do so here and will stay focused on the more immediate aspects of your question.

When each of us die we are subject to what is called a "particular judgment". This judgment determines where are souls go, which will be to heaven, hell or to Purgatory. At this point our human bodies whither and "return to dust". If we die with sins we have not confessed, repented or have not been absolved through the Sacrament of Reconciliation and repaid (fulfilled our penance), our souls are unclean or have the stain of sin on them (figuratively not literally for the soul does not have a physical property) and therefore need to get cleansed (again figuratively). No soul can enter heaven in this unclean state but can still be worthy of heaven. All souls in the Purgatory process of purification will get to heaven, we just don't know how long it will take to be cleansed. If our soul is pure it will go directly to heaven. If our soul is mortally dead, that is, lacks all sanctifying grace, it will go to hell.

So, what happens at the general judgment at the end of the world? Well at this point all those still living at the time and all those souls who previously passed away will be called to a social or general judgment. We will be rejoined with a new body. If we are to go to heaven, we will be joined with a newly glorified body free from pain, suffering, disease and death. Those that are not deemed worthy of heaven by their own actions and choices, will also be rejoined with their bodies but will be subject to an eternal life without a vision or relationship with God. There will be further suffering that may be equivalent to eternal solitary confinement. Please know our particular judgment and the result of the general judgment will be the same.

Randy Alcorn, in his book, *Deception,* provides an imaginative, fictional view of hell that is truly scary in its simplicity and in its stark view of a life without God, of eternal unrelenting anguish. Yet in his books, *Edge of Eternity* and *In Light of Eternity,* Randy Alcon provides an exponentially more rewarding, fulfilling and inviting view of what eternal life in heaven might be like. These descriptions, while fictional, are richly based in scripture. Randy Alcorn helps his readers begin to appreciate what type of an eternally rewarding place heaven, or the New Earth, might be like when you consider we each have a place specifically made for us by a Supreme Being with an unimaginable imagination! He likens all the glory of our current God-made universe, which is mortal and will one day perish, to the knotty and tangled underside of a tapestry. Heaven is the significantly more glorious front side of the tapestry that reveals the full glory of God's overall plan for us! If you have seen the bottom side of a high-quality hand sewn tapestry you can begin to appreciate this analogy! This is a great fictional depiction of the devil and his tactics.

The devil would have us discount how eternally rewarding heaven will be, so we do not value it as much or seek it as fervently as we ought! I encourage all I meet to read C.S. Lewis's, *The Screwtape Letters* (but only after first reading his great work, *Mere Christianity).* There are hundreds of scriptural references to why God made us, what his plans and wishes are for us, and how he has prepared a very special place, uniquely for each one of us that chooses by their life's actions and decisions, to join him in heaven. We reaffirm this belief in the twelfth article of faith in the Apostles Creed.

11. Why do they not talk much about Jesus's childhood in the Gospels?

It is understood Jesus lived to be thirty-three and started his "public life" around the age of thirty. Most of scripture focuses on his early life and his public life for reasons I will cover later in this answer.

So, Joseph married Mary, even though she was already "with child", pregnant, and he was the perfect model of fatherhood as the head of the Holy Family. Like Jesus's early life, we do not hear much about Joseph after the birth of Jesus and certainly nothing more after he is about twelve (the story of finding Jesus in the temple with the knowledgeable Jewish priests and leaders). There is relatively little written about Joseph, but it was believed he was a much older man when he married Mary. Some believe he may have been previously married and had children before his first wife passed away. This would be one explanation for some references to Jesus's brothers and sisters in the Bible, but these references could also have been figurative and not literal.

Remember the Gospel writers did not start writing their Gospels for many decades after Jesus's death and resurrection, at least seventy plus years later. They believed the second coming that Christ promised was imminent and as such they did not feel compelled initially to write Jesus's teachings down until they realized maybe his timeline was much different than they appreciated. Until this time the apostles and fellow disciples of Christ simply repeated Jesus's messages and teachings verbally. The

Gospel writer John even tells us at one point in his writings, "not all that Jesus said and did "have been written here" but was has been written is important to our salvation and has been written so that we might believe in him. Another explanation I have heard for why it took seventy years to start writing the Gospels was that it was at this point in time when the initial eye witnesses to Jesus and his teachings were starting to pass away and there was an appreciation for the need to commit the "Good News", the Gospels, to written form.

So, the message is that Sacred Scripture includes the most important aspects of Jesus's life and his teachings, those parts that are most critical to our knowing Jesus's intended messages, or that which is necessary for our salvation. Many details have been intentionally left out so that we can focus on that which is critical and vital. Absolutely, everything Jesus said and did was very important and had meaning not only for those alive during Jesus's time but for every generation to follow. Jesus was omniscient, all knowing, and therefore was communicating an understanding of how his message was going to being received, understood and in many cases misunderstood, so he said, then would resay and behaved in ways that would help us understand what his intended message was for all of us.

The biblical authors were inspired by God to write what they did and by default, to leave out what they did. Jesus purposely remained out of the limelight or out of public exposure until he was ready to start his public ministry at age thirty, which was also the age Levitical priests formally commenced their practice as priests. On a practical level, the Gospel writers and those that assisted them, did not know Jesus until he started his public life. Luke's Gospel is the most detailed or historical in content about other aspects of Jesus' life, notably his recounting of the Angel Gabriel's visit to Mary and Mary's visit to her cousin Elizabeth. It is understood Luke was not writing from first-hand experience but from interviewing Mary directly.

The key is the Gospel writers understood the focus should be on Jesus's public ministry and his teachings so that is what they did.

12. Why cannot women be priests or leaders of the Catholic Church?

While I used to struggle with this personally, there are very good reasons why the Catholic Church holds the positions it does regarding limiting the ordination of men to the priesthood. There is an even louder clamor today for women to be priests given the lack of men (and women) pursuing religious vocations. This question is covered in a good but general way in the book, *What We Really Want to Know,* by Matthew Francis Pennock (page 168). I used to struggle with this same question and the requirement of priests to be celibate (not marry or have relations with women). I used to wonder if the Son of God became man today instead of over two thousand years ago, would he have had women disciples? When I raised this point with a priest who I knew and trusted to be aligned with Church teaching, he reminded me that Jesus was a rebel, a non-conformist, he constantly challenged the status quo. For example, Jesus dined with tax collectors and harlots; he regularly chastised the pharisees and other Jewish leaders; he claimed and acted as though he had the power to forgive sins…and oh yes, he said he was the Son of God, the promised messiah. So, Jesus did not just pick men to be his initial church leaders out of concern for disturbing the status quo or to conform with the cultural practices of the day.

We must remember a calling to the priesthood is a gift given to us by Jesus Christ. A vocation is a calling by God. Men do not choose to be priests or brothers, nor do women chose to be nuns. Rather they are called by God to this vocation, or to the religious life, and most important, they choose to respond positively to God's call or not. Remember when Peter (known as Simon at the time) responded to Jesus's question of, "who do you say that I am?" with the response, "You are the Messiah, the Son of God", Jesus said, "you did not come to this (conclusion) on your own". He said, "You know this because my Father has revealed it to you." Jesus then went on to change Simon's name to Peter and made him the first priest and the first pope. Priesthood is not a right or an entitlement like human rights or equal rights, it is a calling, and, in turn a positive, willing response, to that call. See Matthew's Gospel for the specific wording and details (Mt 16: 13-20).

Jesus remained celibate while he was on earth and called only men to be his apostles. Jesus's apostles imitated his example by also calling males as priests. Church teaching stresses that sacramental signs, both persons and objects, should represent what they signify by "natural resemblance". The priest is a perceptible sign, "another Christ" (see the *Catechism of the Catholic Church* – read the whole Article 6 starting at section 1539). Therefore, since Christ was a male, and remained unmarried/celibate, so too should the priest be male and unmarried.

I also admit, I did not appreciate the value and challenge of single, celibate priests (and nuns) until I became a parent myself. I can better appreciate how difficult it would be to remain as dedicated to my parishioners as I would need to be if I also had a wife and children to care for. Being a priest is more than a nine-to-five job, it is a full time, twenty-four/seven, sacrificial vocation. Something would suffer mightily if one was both a priest (or a nun) and was also married. You should know that when a priest takes his vows, he commits to loving each one of his flock equally and to the best of his ability. All priests vow to "consecrate themselves with an undivided heart to the Lord".

You can see then the potential natural conflict if priests were also married/non-celibate. It would be hard, on more than a few occasions, for a married priest to put a need of a family member behind, or second to, that of a parishioner. As a married man and father, the priest would be constantly torn between prioritizing the needs of his family with those of his parishioners. As I became more personally active and involved in my local parish of St. Michael's, I developed a much better appreciation for the countless hours with early mornings, late nights and extremely full weekends, our pastor and our associate vicar, maintained...week in and week out! I don't know how they sustained the hectic schedules they did as individuals...and this was without any consideration for responding to the emergency demands and needs of over ten thousand parishioners. I thought as a married man and hard-working father of seven children that I had a demanding schedule. Their schedules were far more demanding, and it was then that I began to appreciate the value and the necessity for unmarried priests, so they could truly live up to their vow of putting the needs of their parishioners first. If they had spouses and children, they would be constantly torn between the demands of family life and the demands of the priesthood. Please know that celibacy dates back to the first apostles but this is a whole separate point that requires a much more detailed explanation.

This is a simplified version of a series of more subtle reasons for why only men should be priests and why they should remain celibate or focused on their vocation and devotion to Christ. When you talk to priests about this subject and their own personal vocational calls, you can begin to understand why this makes sense. A vocation to the priesthood is not something you select but rather you are called to and respond to because you are open to God's will.

One other perspective I was given on this question from a priest on Relevant Radio is that the Church is not an institution, it is a family. All families need a head and the male is the head of the family. This is supported throughout Sacred Scripture and by Christ himself. The little we hear about Joseph, especially in Matthew's Gospel, focuses on his role as the head of the Holy Family and as the protector of Mary and Jesus. As such our pope, bishops and priests are the heads of the various Church families and are to be males. In no way does this diminish or detract from the important role women have in their families and in the Church. The point is, there must be a head of the family, and males are that head.

For more details on these general points but in a more literal prose style, read Fr. John Hardon's, *The Catholic Catechism* and focus in on chapter eleven, *Growth in Holiness – Universal Call to Sanctity*.

13. Does Purgatory exist and is there a scriptural basis for Catholic doctrine on this?

So, for those who want the short version, there are indirect scriptural references in the Bible that clearly support and provide a scriptural basis for "Purgatory". I will touch on a few (1Co 3:15, 1Pe 1:7, 1Mc 12:45-46).

I would also point out that while the existence of Purgatory is a more Catholic doctrinal position, there are other examples of Christian doctrinal positions that similarly lack a specific, direct reference in the Bible. The most notable one is the Christian doctrine on the Trinity. The word "Trinity" does not appear anywhere in the Bible yet all of us Christians who believe that Jesus was the Son of God and who appealed to his Father in heaven multiple times and made multiple references to the Holy Spirit, clearly believe in the doctrine of the Trinity.

First, it might be helpful to point out what Catholics DO NOT believe about Purgatory:

- Catholics do not believe Purgatory is a physical "place" or some middle region between heaven and hell
- Nor do Catholics believe it is some sort of low-grade place where folks who did not sin enough or badly enough to merit eternity in hell go for awhile
- Catholics do not pay to "get out" of Purgatory or "earn days off"
- Catholics do not believe one "atones" for one's sins in Purgatory

The *Catechism of the Catholic Church* states in sections 1030 and 1031 that:

All who die in God's grace and friendship [there are whole other sections that speak to what this means], but still imperfectly purified, are indeed assured of their eternal salvation; but after death they undergo purification, so as to achieve the holiness necessary to enter the joy of heaven. The Church gives the name *Purgatory* to this final purification of the elect, which is entirely different from the punishment of the dammed. The Church formulated her doctrine of faith on Purgatory especially at the Councils of Florence and Trent. The tradition of the Church, by reference to certain texts of scripture, speaks of a cleansing fire:

> *As for certain lesser faults, we must believe that, before the Final Judgment, there is a purifying fire. He who is truth says that whoever utters blasphemy against the Holy Spirit will be pardoned neither in this age nor in the age to come. From*

this sentence we understand certain offenses can be forgiven in this age, but for certain others, in the age to come.

Paul says that if after death, a person's life is found wanting, "that one will suffer loss; the person will be saved, but only as through fire" (1Co 3:15).

This is an interesting passage, because it implies after death, a person whose soul is not perfectly clean and worthy to live in the presence of God can still be saved, but only through a painful process. Would this kind of painful process exist in heaven? Of course not, our souls do not endure pain in heaven. So, what could Paul be talking about? Perhaps he's talking about the chance for purification that does indeed come after death, the process we call Purgatory. Furthermore, this pain is not likely to be a physical bodily pain but possibly more of emotional or psychological pain related to a deeper awareness or understanding of how close we are to eternal happiness but not yet able to experience it. Possibly a deep sense of loneliness or a void accruing from being separated from God.

Catholics do not believe Purgatory is a place but rather a process, a process of purification. The point is nothing impure or blemished with sin can live in God's presence and many of us die with imperfectly reconciled souls, so it makes sense for God to give us an opportunity to make things right after death.

Another scriptural reference is in the Old Testament where we find this passage, which, in reference to praying for the dead, says: "But if he did this with a view to the splendid reward that awaits those that had gone to rest in godliness, it was a holy and pious thought. Thus, he made atonement for the dead that they might be freed from sin" (2Mc 12:45-46).

Do souls in heaven bear sin? Do they need prayer? No and no. Do souls in hell, there by their own choice for eternity, benefit from prayer? Again no. So, if there is only heaven and hell, what purpose would "praying for the dead" serve? None! But it is mentioned and mentioned approvingly, so that suggests once again, God's mercy does not end with physical death.

Our Christian brothers will say Jesus "atoned" for our sins through his death and resurrection so there is no such thing as Purgatory or a need for it. Catholics believe this "atonement" does not eliminate the need for the purification process known as Purgatory.

So, I am not sure if this helps you to understand or to better accept the doctrine of Purgatory, but at least it should help clarify there is indeed a scriptural basis.

14. If someone hurts or offends me, do I have to forgive them, even before they admit they were wrong?

This a very good and important question. Friends and family members have been estranged from one another due to our human propensity to hurt those closest to us and then be very tough on each other in terms of understanding and forgiveness. Arguably the pain or the hurt runs deeper when caused by a good friend or family member. Too often, the tendency is for us to be less forgiving to those closest to us whom we feel have offended or hurt us. Life is messy, and it is a rare family or friendship situation that has not felt the pain of separation or estrangement due to one party feeling they have been wronged by another.

As you may know, two parties can have equal access to the same set of "facts" but come away with very different understandings or interpretations of the implications of these facts (could be a case of selective recall). Ask any detective about the "reliability" of "eyewitness" accounts. We all have unconscious biases or filters that color the way we assess various situations. Therefore, it is not uncommon for us to be in situations where one party feels totally wronged and the other is clueless or feels the other party has totally misunderstood or misrepresented the situation and its implications for the respective parties. These can be barriers to recognizing that you have hurt someone, let alone to requesting or granting forgiveness.

As difficult as it may be for us, Jesus and other saints like St. Stephen showed us the way we are to respond in these situations when we have been wronged by others. Jesus forgave his executioners as they were crucifying him, and St. Stephen forgave those who were stoning him to death while they were stoning him. God rewarded St. Stephen for his forgiving ways by enabling him to fall into a deep sleep as he was being stoned to death. Neither Jesus nor St. Stephen "waited" for the abusing parties to recognize the error of their ways, and to ask for forgiveness before they forgave their persecutors. They did not expect or require their persecutors to admit to, acknowledge, or ask for forgiveness... for actions that were clearly wrong.

So as difficult as it may be, we should not "wait" for the party we believe did us wrong to "ask for forgiveness". We should pray for them and forgive them for their transgression or perceived transgression.

Jesus expanded on the Great Commandment he gave us by adding a still higher level of expectation when he said, "A new command I give you: Love one another. As I have loved you, so you must love one another" (Jn 13:34). So, we are called to not only love as Jesus loved but to forgive as Jesus taught us to forgive by his own example on Good Friday.

Forgiving people who've wronged us is one of the most difficult things God asks us to do. Minor insults and slights can be easier to forgive, but what if the offense against you is so painful that it seems unpardonable? How can you forgive someone who broke your heart or hurt someone you love?

Thankfully, we have the perfect example of forgiveness in Jesus, who, while in agony on the cross, said, "Father, forgive them, they know not what they do" (Lk 23:34). Jesus makes it clear that we must model our forgiveness of others on God's forgiveness of our sins.

Here are a few lines from Scripture in which Jesus talks about the grace of forgiveness and why it's essential:

> "If you forgive others their transgressions, your heavenly Father will forgive you. But if you do not forgive others, neither will your Father forgive your transgressions" (Mt 6:14-15).

"Be on your guard! If your brother sins, rebuke him; and if he repents, forgive him. And if he wrongs you seven times in one day and returns to you seven times saying, 'I am sorry,' you should forgive him" (Lk 17: 3-4).

"Stop judging and you will not be judged. Stop condemning and you will not be condemned. Forgive and you will be forgiven. Give and gifts will be given to you; a good measure, packed together, shaken down, and overflowing, will be poured into your lap. For the measure with which you measure will in return be measured out to you" (Lk 6:37-38).

"Then Peter approaching asked him, "Lord, if my brother sins against me, how often must I forgive him? As many as seven times?" Jesus answered, "I say to you, not seven times but seventy-seven times" (Mt 18:21-22).

And finally, to put it all in perspective:

"While they were eating, Jesus took bread, said the blessing, broke it, and giving it to his disciples he said, "Take and eat; this is my body. Then he took a cup, gave thanks, and gave it to them, saying, "Drink from it all of you, for this is my blood of the covenant, which will be shed on behalf of many for the forgiveness of sins" (Mt 26:26-28).

So, Jesus set the bar for us, he was very clear. We simply cannot hold on to grudges, no matter how painfully we have been hurt. We must turn the other cheek and forgive our transgressors…without waiting for them to acknowledge their wrongdoing, nor for them to ask for forgiveness. A tall order for most of us!

15. Is the Catholic Church against gay rights or gay marriages?

The Church believes all human life should be treated fairly, with respect and dignity but is against the homosexual lifestyle and considers it sinful. One might have homosexual leanings or desires but these, in and of themselves, are not sinful. It is only when we act on these proclivities, that is to engage in same sex relations that it becomes sinful. We are all human and as such we are all weak and susceptible to temptations of the flesh or lust, as well to other sinful activity such gluttony, pride, envy, sloth, greed and wrath. While we have the Sacrament of Reconciliation to repent and be forgiven for our sinful ways, we also must make a commitment to change our lives and to avoid the occasion of sin. It is just as sinful for a man to have sexual relations with another man, or for a woman with another woman, as it is for an unmarried man, or a married man, to have sexual relations with a woman other than his wife or outside of marriage. These are sins against the sixth commandment, thou shall not commit adultery. The sixth commandment is about remaining faithful to God's **natural law** to treat sexual relations as sacred for the purpose of procreation (having children).

Just like a heterosexual person, let us say an unmarried male, must resist urges or desires to have pre-marital sexual relations with a woman, so to, a person must resist urges he/she might feel to have sexual relations with another person of their same sex or to self-gratify oneself.

The Catholic Church teaches that having homosexual relations is a mortal or grave sin against God, but the Church reaches out and loves all men and women and does not look down on homosexuals but teaches against a homosexual lifestyle. A great, loving, non-judgmental approach to the topic of homosexuality—and to many other aspects of sexuality, is covered extremely well by Christopher West in his book, *Theology of the Body for Beginners*. It is a thin book--and amazing. *Theology of the Body for Beginners* explains from the very beginning of creation that God had a plan for us, (i.e. our souls and our bodies) that is so much more than the physical pleasures of this world. It is beautifully and logically explained as only John

Paul II could have done through the inspiration of the Holy Spirit. His explanations of God's love and God's design, not the "rules" is inspiring! *Theology of the Body* in one form or another is fast becoming a Pre-Cana requirement in many Catholic parishes for soon to be married couples. It is also being introduced at the high school level in many Catholic high schools as a key part of instruction in morality. There are several Theology of the Body for Teens versions including one by Jason Evert that are marvelous. *Theology of the Body* is a must-read for all Christians, atheists… all of us. Maybe your parents will add this to their library, and you can read it when you are ready to?

Many say homosexuality is genetic or a result of one's natural desires and as such is intrinsic to who we are as humans. The argument then follows that if this is part of our human natures and God made man, then it cannot be wrong or sinful to actively engage in homosexual behavior since God made us this way. I will not even attempt to get into the genetic issue for it is truly a moot point to both the logic and to overall rationale of the Church's position.

First, to the logic issue. To imply simply that since God made us, including persons who have selected a gay lifestyle, that living a homosexual lifestyle should not be a sin, is to ignore a fundamental quality that separates man (homo sapiens) from all other life forms. That is, God gave us things that no other plants, animals or insects have. He gave us special immortal souls (all living things have souls, but they are mortal, remember God made us "above" or superior to all other life forms), a free will, an intellect and a conscience. So yes, God created man, but he gave us the individual ability to reason and to make individual choices or decisions on how we live our lives'.

Many exercise their free wills, most of the time, in ways that are good. However, because we are all human, we will at times choose to do evil or to sin. We succumb to temptation to the weaknesses we have as humans and to the power of the devil. Does this make us evil individuals? No, but it does make us a weak and sinful people. Is the Catholic Church then implying that homosexuals are evil? No not evil, but yes, the Church's position is that homosexual relations, masturbation, use of contraceptives and other "unnatural" sexual acts are wrong or sinful, they are against the natural order, against God's plan for us when he created us. I struggled with the right word to use (too bad we all do not speak Greek which often has a multiplicity of words for everyone word in English to provide more exact meaning. PLEASE DO NOT take the word UNNATURAL literally. Read Fr. Hardon's description below.

But I have still not told you what about homosexual relations is sinful in the eyes of God. Fr. John A. Hardon, in his book, *The Question and Answer Catholic Catechism* says, "masturbation and homosexual relations are contrary to the will of God because by their very nature they are selfish actions which cannot fulfill the divinely ordained purpose of our reproductive powers."

I would also strongly encourage you to read Fr. Hardon's, *The Catholic Catechism* (pages 353-356). In short, what the Church is saying is we have an obligation to use our reproductive powers in very specific and directed ways all leading directly to the possibility of a certain outcome, that is, procreation, or the birth of a child. So even though we have the need for emotional releases and the desire to fulfill desires we might have, this does not mean we can do this without limits or restrictions. Just like we cannot simply act whenever we want, or however we want, whenever we feel the need or get the urge, such as when we are hungry, want something new, etc. One could make the same argument about heterosexual behavior. Heterosexual males and females have urges or desires relative to members of their opposite sex. Whether the persons are married or single, they cannot simply act on every desire or urge that comes upon them. These urges or desires must be channeled, directed or controlled and behavior must be socially and morally acceptable. The same applies to homosexual urges and desires. The Catholic Church holds many positions regarding sexual behavior that are not popular in today's world for other Christian faiths and for many Catholics. These include, in addition to condoning ONLY heterosexual relationships, the Church's position against abortion, against the use of contraceptives, and the inability to remarry following divorce if the former spouse is still alive, and many other positions.

So yes, the Catholic Church is opposed to gay or homosexual relations and to gay marriages if those marriages result in homosexual relations. The Church does not judge or condemn homosexuals just like they do not judge or condemn any of us who let our desires rule our decisions. This is known as concupiscence or a conflict between desire and reason or otherwise known as an unruly passion or sexual desire.

I appreciate I cannot in this forum, fully cover this point. Please read the references provided or seek out other Catholic based sources for a better, more detailed explanation.

16. When you die, do you see what is happening on earth?

There is not a simple yes or no to your question but for clarity I will say that those in heaven have an awareness of what is going on right now on earth. I chose my words carefully here as this wording is backed by the Catholic Church and by Sacred Scripture.

After death, your human body withers to dust (along with your eyes) but your soul lives on and goes to one of three places, heaven, hell or Purgatory. But your soul is spiritual in nature and can still see in a sense or be aware. The Catholic Church also holds that at the Final Judgment, our souls will be reunited with our glorified bodies which includes a body with eyes.

There are two different types of sight in heaven: first, the sight of the mind or soul (you need to understand that we are more than just human bodies but that we are spirits as well via our souls but this is very heady stuff to get into and helps if you know Hebrew and Greek as it relates to things like psyche, conscience and intellect, which helps us explain and understand why our "souls" are what makes us different from other living creatures) and, second, actual physical sight.

Scripture tells us we will see God "face to face" (1Co 13:12; Rev 22:3-4; 1Jn 3:2; CCC 1023). However, this sight will be different from the sight experienced with our material bodies. Matthew Pinto uses the example:

> If I ask you "Do you see what I mean?" you are really "seeing" with your mind. This is similar to how we will know God (or see God immediately after our particular judgment) because God the Father does not have a body (Jn 4:24; CCC 370). We will experience God even more closely than we experience our own thoughts. We will know God in a much more intimate way and our experiences will be realized in a much different way.
>
> We will experience God without having anything block the experience (Rev 9:15). Even thoughts in our minds are currently "blocks" to "the real thing" because they are simply mental representations.
>
> The second type of sight is the physical sight we experience on earth. At the end of time, after the general resurrection (and Final Judgment), we will literally see Jesus, Mary, and the saints, and our glorified bodies will be rejoined to our souls. However, our "sight" will be different from our current experience because we will see God in all the creatures we gaze upon (1Co 15:41-44; CCC 1052). And because God wants all of us to be happy in heaven, we will surely see everything necessary for our happiness.

This is also consistent with what Fr. Hardon tells us the Lord promises us in Sacred Scripture. The "just" on the Final Judgment Day will have two rewards to look forward to: "possession of God and enjoyment of creatures".

Pinto also reminds us: "Based on the doctrine of the Communion of Saints, we also believe the saints in heaven do have some knowledge (sight) of those on earth" (Rev 6:9-10; Heb 12:1). We will know and understand the human experience much more deeply than we do now".

17. If Jesus, God, and the Holy Spirit are all one person, then why don't we say Jesus, or the Holy Spirit created the world/universe/earth?

Your general question could apply in many other ways or to many other events. The concept of the Holy Trinity is a difficult one to wrap our human intellects around yet the basis for the doctrine of the Holy Trinity is well documented throughout Sacred Scripture. The word "Trinity" does not appear anywhere in the Bible, nor does the word "Purgatory" or the word "incarnation" yet all these doctrines have been a part of the rich tradition of the Catholic Church for centuries. In fact, our protestant friends accept the doctrines on the Holy Trinity and of the Incarnation (the Son of God made man, or the "Word" made flesh). Many Protestants, however, do not accept our Catholic doctrine on Purgatory.

We believe there are three very distinct persons in our one God. They are all one in the same God, but each has a distinct nature or essence. The divine persons do not share the one divinity among themselves but each of them is God whole and entire. Section 254 and 255 of the *Catechism of the Catholic Church* instructs us that:

> *The divine persons are really distinct from one another.* "God is one but not solitary." "Father," "Son," and "Holy Spirit" are not simply names designating modalities of the divine being, for they really are distinct from one another. "He is not the Father who is the Son, nor is the Son he who is the Father, nor is the Holy Spirit he who is the Father or the Son." They are distinct from one another in their relations of origin: "It is the Father who generates, the Son who is begotten, and the Holy Spirit who proceeds." The Divine Unity is Triune."
>
> *The divine persons are relative to one another.* Because it does not divide the divine unity, the real distinction of the persons from one another resides solely in the relationships which relate them to one another: "In the relational names of the persons, the Father is related to the Son, the Son to

the Father, and the Holy Spirit to both. While they are called three persons in view of their relations, we believe in one nature or substance." "Because of that unity the Father is wholly in the Son and the Holy Spirit; the Son is wholly in the Father and wholly in the Holy Spirit; the Holy Spirit is wholly in the Father and wholly in the Son."

So, since it is the Father who "generates", we associate all creation with God the Father and since God the Son is begotten, we associate Jesus with God the Son and since the Holy Spirit proceeds, we associate our souls and our gifts of faith with the Holy Spirit. However, since they are one, we would not be totally incorrect to relate certain outcomes to either of the three persons in one God, but we might be clearer or more correct in our communication to relate the appropriate outcomes with one of the three particular persons in our One God.

I fear I may have made this more confusing to you, but Trinitarian doctrine is not easy to explain let alone wrap our heads around. Please read sections 232-260 in your copy of the *Catechism of the Catholic Church* for more details.

18. **If God knows what is going to happen in the future, why does he test you on your faith if he knows the result? And a related question, "If God knows everything that is going to happen in the future do we really have free wills?"**

   Someone else asked, "Does God know what is going to happen before it does? If yes, why was God so mad when Adam and Eve sinned if he knew it would happen?"

First, God did not put us on this earth to test us. He made us to know him, to love him, to serve him and to be happy with him in Heaven. If you read one of the two creation accounts in the Book of Genesis, you will find that after God had made all else, he made man and women, superior to all others because He made us "like" himself and gave us dominion over all the other animals he had previously created. The part that makes us unique and "God-like" is our immortal souls, which means they never die, they are eternal like God. Along with our unique immortal souls, he gave us free wills with the intellect to exercise our free wills'. We can make conscience choices and not just act based on instinct or on a "survival mode". Animals have souls, but they are mortal they do not have a "God-like" quality of immortality and while they have some intellect, they are more instinctual. Animals do not have consciences like those of human beings. When you get older you may want to delve into all the Greek and Hebrew aspects of human nature as defined in Sacred Scripture which goes beyond just body and soul.

And yes, God is omniscient or "all knowing" so he knows exactly what choices we are going to make before we ever make them. Before we are even born and reach the point when we can even make any of the choices in question, he knows what choices we will make. "Before I formed you in the womb, I knew you" (Jer 1:5).

However, just because he knows what our decision will be, that does not mean that we do not make those choices of our own free wills'. Our lives are not predetermined or predestined, they are totally up to each one of us and the decisions we make. He does not directly change our minds and "cause" us to make one decision versus another. One of our uniquely human qualities given us by God is our "free will", to consciously decide on taking one path versus another...then we must live with the consequences of exercising our free will. In some cases, these are minor decisions such as going to one movie versus another. Other times it could be a decision to be obedient to our parent's instructions...or not, or to respect our date or our spouses wishes...or not. These decisions can have more profound consequences.

As Catholics, we believe that by having faith in God, by believing in him and attempting to live our lives' as consistently with that belief as we possibly can, we can achieve eternal life. We cannot "make-up" for our sins or the sin of Adam and Eve and we cannot "earn" our way into heaven, but we do have an obligation to recognize our human failings, to reconcile ourselves with God through the Sacrament of Reconciliation and to amend our lives to try not to repeat our sinful ways. Jesus taught us how to pray and how to live our lives'. He gave us the Beatitudes as a balance to the Ten Commandments. The commandments are more about the things we should "not do" (they mostly begin with "Thou shall not" and they mostly define potential sins of commission. The Beatitudes address the things we should DO in our daily lives and failure to do those things or order are lives' that way, can result in sins of omission.

God knows we are human and that we will err, repeatedly. God sent his Son to conquer sin and death, to open the gates of heaven and to give us the opportunity to positively use our free wills to make choices consistent with how Jesus taught us to live and act. This is how we can have a confident assurance that as baptized, and then practicing Catholics, we can look forward to an eternity with God. If we consciously reject God and his teachings, we are choosing hell or an eternity without God.

He was more saddened and disappointed by Adam and Eve's decision to disobey his one command then he was mad. He is disappointed anytime any one of us makes a bad decision. The devil tempts us and encourages us to sin, but he cannot "make" us sin. We must choose this on our own. Thankfully Jesus wiped out the effects of Original Sin and thankfully he is a most loving, merciful and forgiving God. God will love us just as much, regardless of how many times we sin or how serious our sins may be. Also, we cannot increase God's love for us by doing kind acts, praying more, or participating more frequently in the sacraments…although these are all good things to do!

He gave us the ability to reconcile our sinful natures with him through the Sacrament of Reconciliation and he gives us the sacraments and taught us to pray so we can use these gifts and their attendant graces to avoid the occasion of sin and to make more good decisions than bad ones. Gospel from Luke includes a story about the shepherd that left his herd of ninety-nine sheep to go after the one lost sheep and upon finding the lost sheep, was more joyful about finding the one lost sheep then he was about having the ninety-nine righteous sheep who did not stray. Jesus loves us more than we can know. I personally believe the other ninety-nine were not all that righteous and Jesus is that much more joyous when we recognize our weaknesses, our lack of full righteousness and return to the fold. Sorry my personal view!

So, by making us superior to plants and animals with free wills and intellects, we have the ability to make good or bad choices. There are always consequences for every choice we make. Some are good, and some are bad…both the choices and the consequences.

19. Do animals go to heaven?

So, my answer would depend on who is asking the question just like if someone were to ask, "where to babies come from?" So, if a young child was asking me this question, I would say yes, you will see animals in heaven and that babies come from God. That is I would keep my answer simple. However, for a more discerning, more mature questioner I would want to provide a more in-depth answer. Surprised?

One of two promises made to us by the Lord is that the "just" on the Final Judgment Day will have two rewards to look forward to: "possession of God and enjoyment of creatures". So yes, animals or pets as well as other plants, fishes etc. will be part of our heavenly experience as part of the new glorified earth, a new creation However, these other creatures who have mortal souls unlike our immortal ones, will have a much different heavenly experience from what we humans, made in His "image and likeness" will experience.

Indirectly, there is a whole book written on this topic that I enjoyed on multiple levels. The most important one is that it gave me a broader view of heaven then I ever appreciated before. This is another book by Randy Alcorn, "In Light of Eternity". While Randy Alcorn is not Catholic or clarifying Catholic dogma, he does cite numerous scriptural references that essentially paints a picture of a glorified earthly experience without the limitations, pains and weaknesses of our current mortal existence on earth. Maybe an even better version of the "Garden of Eden" before Adam and Eve sinned. He goes on to describe how it is conceivable that animals could be part of our heavenly experience.

One thing the Catholic Church is clear on is that human beings were created unique to all other living creatures in that we were born with souls, with intellects, and free wills. Plants and animals were not similarly blessed. Given this we will have a unique opportunity to be happy in heaven or we can choose to not accept God's gift of salvation. Plants and animals do not have this ability.

The devil wants us to accept a less than exciting view of what heaven may really be like. He would have us believe we will just be lifeless spirits floating aimlessly around or spending every minute in prayer adoring God. Scripture tells us that after the Final Judgment, we will be reunited with our glorified bodies. Randy Alcorn imagines an even more physical, earth like, interactive heavenly experience that will be an unbelievable enhancement to the mortal earthly experience we know today.

Scripture tells us our heavenly experiences will not all be the same and will reflect how well we lived our faith, served God, while on earth. Extensions of that thinking are that we will experience plants and animals, especially pets if they were important to you when we are in heaven. He further suggests our experience in heaven will be a dynamic and ever changing one. For example, we might be able to see our grandparents as we knew them before they passed away and yet also as they were as teenagers. We are promised that God has prepared a place for each one of us, we cannot begin to imagine how wonderful that place might be. However, if pets were important to us on earth there is a very good chance these animals will be part of our heavenly experience.

Animals have brains and instincts but not our other uniquely human attributes of a free will, a conscience, or an eternal soul. Since they do not have free wills, they cannot discern right from wrong, they cannot sin because they cannot choose to sin. So, an animal killing a human being would not be a sin. We use our intellects to reason and our conscience guides the decisions we make on how we exercise our free will. However, when we die, it is our soul that will live on while our bodies' whither and turn to dust (with the exception of Mary who was assumed into heaven body and soul to preserve the perfect vessel that enabled Jesus, the Son of Man to assume a human nature and be born. Mary was the New Testament superior to Eve and to the Ark of the Covenant.). Our soul is a spiritual, free and immortal substance individually created by God and infused into the human body at conception (Fr. John S. Hardon's, *The Catholic Question and Answer Catechism*).

Our soul is our spiritual essence given to us by God while our parents give us our human essence, and both occur at the time we are conceived in our mother's womb. Since animals cannot reason (use an intellect), do not have a conscience and cannot exercise a free will they cannot commit sins. While as living creatures they have souls, their souls are very different from ours. Our souls are immortal, they never die, while animals' souls are mortal. Since animals do not have souls like ours and cannot sin, they cannot be born with Original Sin, but they also will not have the same experience of heaven that we will enjoy.

20. How is it that the Pope does not make mistakes?

I expect you are asking how a human could, even if he is a Pope, be infallible? However, the Pope is only infallible, without error, in matters of dogmatic positions when he speaks "ex cathedra" or "from the throne". He is human and can make bad decisions, can sin and make errors in all other areas of his life. He could fail a math test, a foreign language or history, or even a constitutional test, but he cannot err in matters of official dogmatic Church positions. The Pope does not act alone when taking a dogmatic position. He relies on the magisterium, the teaching body of the church, and the Holy Spirit to help guide him. However, this does not mean that the Pope's choice of words he uses to convey the teaching will be ideal or that his timing or that his method of communicating it will be done in the best way.

21. Are exorcisms real? If yes, how do demons get inside you or possess you and why do they do so? Do devils only possess Christians?

The need for exorcisms is very real, they are performed more frequently than one might think, and they vary in type.

Fr. John A. Hardon's, *The Catholic Catechism* (pages 87-90), reminds us that the Gospel's are filled with descriptive narratives about the activities and strategies of the devil. Time and again Christ drove out demons from people who were possessed. St. Mark's Gospel is particularly detailed in the number of exorcisms performed by Christ. Not only are the Gospels explicit about the existence and machinations of evil spirits but they also state their number is legion which is a synonym for an immense multitude. So, the devil and his minions are real, and they have been exorcised by Christ and his delegates.

Now, as to the how and why? The devil's purpose is to tempt and seduce, to lead us astray from God. The devil's activity or desire to tempt is generally proportionate to a person's proximity to God. So then, it is understandable that the devil would focus on Christians versus non-Christians but not exclusively so. Please know that Lucifer was a fallen angel, and as such has supernatural abilities which include possession. God's purpose is always good, but he permits the devil to tempt us but never beyond our strength. So, God permits evil with the intention that by resisting the devil we draw naturally closer to him. God's permission of evil is exemplified in the biblical Book of Job. We may not fully appreciate how God's permission and use of evil fits with his overall plan of salvation for us, but he does not cause evil, but he does permit evil.

The devil shapes his temptations and deceitful ways to best fit the characteristics or vulnerabilities of each of his targets. Fr. Hardon writes,

"There are such things as possession, when the devil exerts his influence over a person by an inner control over his body; and obsession, when he attacks their bodies from the outside. However, the victim's liberty of soul always remains intact."

Possession, like other attacks or approaches by the devil, are always intended to deceive the victim and to turn the person away from God. The devil is extremely cunning and knows how to exploit our weak points. Therefore, we need to take advantage of the sacraments to gain more sanctifying grace and increase our resources to make good decisions and resist temptation. I would encourage you to read C.S. Lewis's *"The Screwtape Letters"*. This is a book about Satan corresponding back and forth with other devils about the continued efforts to corrupt their assigned humans. A very interesting and thought provoking read!

22. When the world ends, will the devil die or will he live forever?

Satan, a.k.a. St. Lucifer, is a fallen angel and never had and never will have a human body or any mortal qualities. God permits the devil to continue to work his evil ways, to tempt us and to lead us astray and will continue to let him do so until the Final Judgment Day. This is a cost of our gift of free wills. However, on the Final Judgment Day, God will banish the devil to hell forever, along with all of us who chose the devil over God, Satan will no longer have any power or influence over us, those that are rewarded with eternal life in heaven. So, the devil will "live" eternally just like all the other angels. However, his influence over us will come to an end!

23. What is the Catholic Church's view on evolution? How could Adam and Eve have been the source of all the different races of mankind?

Books have been written on these topics, so I will not be able to do it full justice nor do I fancy myself an expert on Creation, Evolution, the Big

Bang and other related scientific theories. The Catholic Church's position is that God created the earth, plants, animals and that he created man (homo sapiens, so both males and females). He created man in his image and likeness. However, the Church does not take a position on the exact "how" of creation, the Church leaves this to science. It is our souls that God creates in each one of us and it is our souls that most closely reflect his image and likeness. Why you ask? Because our souls are the only part of our essence that is immortal like he is, they will never die. While our parents are responsible for our human aspects or natures, it is God (through the Holy Spirit) who is specifically responsible for our god-like natures, our souls.

However, I believe, as does the Catholic Church, that one can believe in Creation Theory (Church's position) and still leave room for other scientific theories, certainly for the Big Bang Theory and many aspects of Evolution Theory. The Big Bang Theory was developed by a Jesuit priest, Fr. Georges Lemaître! Fr. Lemaître's work provided the key problem-solving formula for Einstein's Theory of Relativity...talk about religion co-operating with science! Creation and evolution theories can co-exist as explanations for our origins... they are not necessarily in conflict with one another. The Catholic Church draws the line on accepting evolutionary theory up to the point it supports "random mutations" for the Church believes our creation was a totally designed or planned outcome. In fact, there are many scientific arguments that support the belief that our universe could not have just been a random act. I encourage you to check out Fr. Spitzer's *Credible Catholic* modules on science and faith. The key is for the respective disciplines of science and religion/faith or the Bible to stay within their relative areas of strength. So, as it relates to the origin of our universe, of human life, science is best able to address the questions of "When?" and "How?" we came to be and religion to address the questions of "Who/" made us and "Why?" we were made.

Alright, I will quit rambling and get to the answer! So, could the Book of Genesis, in its description of creation, have aspects to it that are not one hundred percent scientifically factual? The answer, like for so many other details throughout the Bible, is yes. In fact, the Book of Genesis is a poetic book, not a historical one. However, that does not mean the messages God intended when he inspired the biblical authors to write, is any less true or accurate. For example, does it really matter if God created the world in six days? In fact, the calendar was not even invented back then and, time for God as a supreme, immortal being, is not what it is to us mortals. What to us is a day or twenty-four hours, could be a millennium for God. This detail (not "fact"), like so many other "details" in the Bible is not what is important. What is important, is that the Church teaches, and we as Catholics believe, that God created both the world and man as described above.

So, was there a physical place known as the Garden of Eden, where there was no pain, suffering, disease, illness or even physical discomfort? Was there a man named Adam and a woman made from Adam's rib and if yes, what color were they?

As I stated, the Book of Genesis is not a historical book, it is a poetic book. I want you to remember that everything in the Bible should not be taken as one-hundred percent factual or historical (don't confuse factual with accurate, but more to come on this, read on). Jesus spoke in parables or stories to convey his messages to a people who were relatively uneducated. He had to speak in simple terms. Also, much of the Bible, particularly the Old Testament, was derived by finally writing down what had been communicated verbally from one generation to another. This method of communication is going to have difficulty keeping all the details straight. However, please know the biblical authors were ALL inspired by the Holy Spirit, the third person in the Trinity.

Please also remember that the Book of Genesis has two very different creation accounts or "stories". You should read Genesis to understand what these two accounts are and how different they are. Does that make one right and the other wrong? Does it mean that neither are right? NO, to both questions.

The Church does not attempt to resolve the many questions about Adam and Eve's race, color or creed, or even their actual existence as literally referenced in the Bible. The Church leaves these questions to science to address.

However, the truth of the message behind Adam, Eve, and the Garden, it fervently supports. That is, that God created man and the whole universe; that man (and woman) were first born without original sin but then exercised their free wills and demonstrated their human nature by sinning; that this act of sin required God the Son to become incarnate in the form of Jesus to die and open the gates of heaven; and so much more. Remember, focus on the meaning of the Word, not on scriptural details.

Does it really matter what color Adam and Eve were; if there was a literal place called the Garden of Eden. I don't think so.

The key is in understanding what the biblical authors' messages were intended to be and what they mean for us living today (we rely on the Pope in union with the magisterium of the church for guidance and direction here). I cannot stress enough, do not get hung up on the details in the Bible, focus on the big picture, what is God's message to us? What did he intend us to learn or do as a result of the biblical details and stories used to convey his message?

Biblical scholar Daniel B. Wallace points out in Lee Strobel's book, *The Case for the Real Jesus,* which outlines a hierarchal foundation for the Bible, that the Bible is first an *inspired* book in that it was written by men who wrote in their own words, with their own abilities and limitations, but they wrote what God inspired them to write. In short, God would have said, "That is what I wanted to be written". He says secondly, it is an *infallible* book meaning the Bible is true in what it *teaches*. This means the Bible is one hundred percent true/accurate in terms of delivering the message God intended. Finally, he reminds us that as a historical book, the Bible is *inerrant* in that it is one hundred percent true regarding the historical issues that it *touches* or relates to, but NOT, that it is one hundred percent historically accurate. So, just because there are conflicting details in various biblical accounts of the same event, or just because there may be details that are not historically accurate, it does not mean you "throw the baby out with the bathwater", you do not discount the entire Bible. The fact that the four gospel writers do not recount events and details of Jesus's life and teachings in exactly the same way lends credibility to their authenticity.

Now, as long as this answer already is, I still feel compelled to continue and address my view of the weaknesses of scientific theory. None of these theories adequately address the philosophical "First Cause" question. That is, if there was a big bang, or if man evolved totally from an ape or some other life form, who or what "caused" the bang, or the "things" that created the "bang" or who created the initial life form that we supposedly evolved from (the first ape or whatever that initial life form was, no matter how crude, or how complex)? Evolutionary scientists agree there are large periods of time in man's history they cannot fully explain or account for. No single theory provides a complete, firm answer as to how our complex universe with all its life forms originated and how those forms changed over time (including how the various races we have came to be). All scientists agree "matter cannot be created, nor destroyed (we can change its molecular structure or visible form by burning, freezing, blowing it up, etc, but we never fully destroy it). So how or where did the very first form or "matter" come from?

There had to be an Uncaused, First Cause (you will get into this in a college level philosophy course, I know you are pumped and can hardly wait!) of a supreme or supernatural nature. The Church believes it is this supreme being that is the First Cause of the universe and of man. We as Catholics believe God was and still is this First Cause, this Supreme Being. So, God could have started (been the First Cause) the Big Bang by creating the things that banged and/or enabling their ability to "bang", if he did not actually directly cause them to bang. If all else followed from this through some great set of evolutionary cycles, would not God still be our "creator"? Does this not enable both creation and evolution theories to co-exist in harmony? I say, of course it does, but I also appreciate that I have greatly simplified things here, but I must move on. However, if scientific theorists at least buy-in to this argument, then we are only debating how MUCH direct intervention God had and on how many of the details in Genesis we accept as fact. Creation theories can explain all that has occurred (even if it is simplified or harder to accept scientifically, but also remember that no one scientific theory has adequately explained our origins.

24. Why can't we remarry after divorce in the Catholic Church?

The Catholic Church's position is that previously married Christians and Catholics who have living spouses cannot get re-married until their spouse dies. Jesus gave the answer to your question when he said, "for this reason a man will leave his father and mother and the two shall become as one. So, they are no longer two but one. No human being must separate what God has joined together" *(Mt 19:3-9).*

So married couples can separate and get divorced (especially when there is abuse or other strong negative factors for one of the spouses or for the children), but they cannot re-marry unless the marriage was "unlawful". In simple terms an unlawful marriage is one based on a lie or a substantive flaw. Catholics can petition their parish priest to have the priest submit a formal request to a special tribunal to have the marriage evaluated for its "lawfulness". If the marriage is found to be unlawful, it is annulled which is as though the marriage never took place at all (since it was based on a lie or a substantive flaw, the marriage never occurred in the eyes of God).

So as a Catholic, or even as a Christian marrying in a Catholic or a Christian Church, the betrothed man and woman vow in the presence of God, the Church, and the priest or minister, who act as God's witnesses during the Sacrament of Matrimony, commit themselves to each other "until death do them part". What God joins; no man can separate. In the other six sacraments, the priest or bishop performs the rite, he baptizes, he confirms, he lays hands etc. In the Sacrament of Matrimony, the priest does not actually marry the couple, the couple marries themselves through their exchange of vows and the priest acts as a witness. The couple commits to each other to be with each other for the rest of their lives and to help each other, and any children they bring into the world, to reach eternal life with God. The couple make a solemn, permanent covenant with one another.

Catholics and as well as other Christian denominations believe that a divorce is spiritually impossible. This also applies to Christians/Catholics who had only a civil marriage rite. So even though a couple may get divorced in a civil court outside of a church, in the eyes of God and the Church, they are still married. (Ro 7:2-3; 1Co 7:10-11, CCC 2382).

The only time a "married" person could get divorced and remarried is if the original marriage was annulled. If a marriage is annulled, it was as though the marriage never took place. While there are many specific examples or justifiable reasons for the annulment, they all fall under the category of the original marriage being "unlawful" or based on a lie or a substantive flaw. Annulments are granted by a Church court (called a tribunal) when it is determined that no valid marriage exists between a couple. This is due to the lack of some necessary element at the time of the marriage by one or both parties: a lack of true consent, the capacity to marry or proper form (see CCC 1629). Examples include, one of the persons was previously married; one of the persons acted under duress; one was mentally incapable of the making a legitimate covenant; one substantively lied, etc.

Some believe the significantly high number of annulments in the US is an indication that the annulment process is flawed or abused. At the end of the day, if the previously married couple lies or abuses the annulment process then they are still married. A more justifiable view, of this high US annulment rate versus other countries is that we as Americans are far more litigious and take "obeying the law", far more seriously than in other countries. Many persons/couples that could qualify for an annulment in other countries simply don't bother do get one because they don't value it enough, don't want to go through the time and effort, or do not want to endure the emotional stress involved. The person(s) must basically admit their wedding covenant was flawed and that once special day, never took place, in the legitimate sense of what the wedding day was all about.

I can understand how Catholics might have difficulty fully embracing this teaching, especially if one spouse totally disrespected the other in such a way that they could no longer live together. The disrespected spouse is put in a very difficult position. Therefore, dating couples, before they get engaged, need to seriously consider the importance of the marital covenant and its permanent nature. A vocational decision like this is one of the most important decisions a human being will have to make in his or her life. It is very important to really talk with each other, ask each other the important questions about what they value and expect from a marriage…well before you get engaged, let alone get married.

On a personal level, I did not follow what I now know to be good advice. It was only after I was engaged that I found out my fiancée was reticent to have children and maybe would want only one child, two at most! I was one of fifteen children, and while I was open to whatever number of children God sent us, I was hoping it would be more than one or two. One of the most painful decisions I had to make was to call off our engagement because it was clear to me that we were too far apart on a very critical area of married life. Out of respect for our differences and the importance of same, I felt I had only one choice but to call off the engagement.

25. Why can't we as Catholics get married in another place, other than a Catholic Church?

The Church prefers a couple to be married, not only in a Catholic Church but also in the couple's own parish church (or in one of the two parties' parish church if they do not have a joint parish, or if one of the two is a non-Catholic). Can there be exceptions? Yes, just like there can be exceptions for a weekday or Sunday mass to be celebrated outside. However, these require special approval by the local bishop, and these are very rare!

Catholics must marry in accordance with "canonical form". This means they are required to have a Catholic wedding ceremony, conducted by either the pastor or another priest deputed by him. If a Catholic wishes to marry a non-Catholic, in a non-Catholic wedding ceremony, which obviously would not be held inside a Catholic church, he must obtain permission from the diocesan bishop in advance. To receive such permission, it must be shown that having a regular Catholic wedding, held in a Catholic church by the pastor or another deputed priest, will present grave difficulties. To cite a common example, if the family of the non-Catholic party is vehemently anti-Catholic, they might refuse to attend the wedding if it is held in a Catholic church. In such a case, the bishop may grant permission to have a non-Catholic wedding elsewhere for the sake of maintaining family harmony.

Canon law states that a marriage between two Catholics, or between a Catholic and a baptized non-Catholic, is to be celebrated in the parish church, although permission can be granted for it to be held in a different Catholic Church or chapel. If two Catholics wish, for example, to be married in a Catholic ceremony not in the parish church, but in the Catholic chapel on their college campus, the bishop can-and in practice, frequently does, approve their request. Occasionally a very tiny parish church may be too small to accommodate all the guests at a large wedding, and permission is obtained to have the wedding in a different, bigger Catholic parish church.

For a Catholic wishing to get married outdoors on a beach, in a park, in a garden, or while sky diving, the law thus far is very restrictive. But the following paragraph may at first glance provide some hope for an alternative: it notes, the bishop <u>can</u> allow a Catholic marriage to be celebrated in another suitable place. Strictly speaking, therefore, it is not impossible under canon law for two Catholics to get married in a Catholic ceremony in a rose garden; if there is nothing intrinsically unsuitable about the location. In contrast, U.S. bishops, have stated in the past that getting married at Disneyland is unacceptable, because they hold that this secular entertainment environment is not a suitable place to celebrate the Catholic Sacrament of Matrimony.

It sounds like all you must do is get approval from the diocesan chancery to have the priest officiate at your wedding in some other location instead of the parish church, right? While, that may be implied by the canon, in actual practice, securing that approval is not so easy.

Church law leaves the decision up to the diocesan bishop. And while I do not have direct knowledge, one priest source I used said there are only very rare instances where a bishop will grant permission and if there is a very good practical reason why the marriage could not take place in a local Catholic Church.

The bishop, in contrast, can and undoubtedly will argue that requiring a wedding to be performed in church is fully in keeping with the fundamental spiritual nature of the occasion. A wedding ceremony entails the conferral and reception of a sacrament. It thus involves far more than mere sentiment, beautiful flowers, and romantic wedding photos taken under a rose trellis. It is important to maintain the sense of the sacred, because that is exactly what a marriage ceremony is-a sacred, sacramental occasion. A bishop who is concerned that the faithful of his diocese keep in mind the central spiritual components of a wedding (as opposed to its cosmetic outward appearances), will quite naturally object to the notion that a Catholic marriage be celebrated outside of a Catholic church. If the very notion of holding a Catholic wedding outside of church is so objectionable for theological reasons, why does the law even permit the possibility? Keep in mind that the Code of Canon Law is applicable all over the globe, and there may be political or other unique circumstances elsewhere in which holding a wedding in a Catholic church is either impossible or inadvisable.

Interestingly, there are a few known cases here in the U.S. where bishops have granted permission for Catholics to marry in a place other than a church, in the presence of a Catholic priest. All of them, however, have involved at least one spouse who was a celebrity. Actors, rock stars, politicians and well-known business executives who get married must contend with the need for privacy. We all know tabloid journalists will go to great lengths to "crash" a movie star's wedding, snap a photo of the bride's dress and get a good look at the invited guests, to see whether there are any more famous faces present. This is naturally a scenario that the couple want to avoid, no matter what faith they profess! If at least one of the pair is Catholic, and they sincerely want to marry in a Catholic ceremony, they may ask the bishop for permission for the wedding to take place in a more private location. Their guards can presumably secure a private residence, or perhaps one wing of a hotel, more reasonably and safely than they could in a Catholic church, which by its nature is generally open to all who wish to enter it. In these highly unusual cases, approval has been given for a Catholic priest to conduct a Catholic wedding ceremony in a building other than a Catholic church. We may assume, however, that efforts are made by the clergy to ensure as much as possible that the sacredness of the occasion, and the spiritual importance of the spouses' exchange of vows, are kept in the forefront.

In a society where, non-Catholic marriage ceremonies include vows being exchanged while scuba or sky diving, the church is trying to emphasize the seriousness and sacredness of the matrimonial commitment and the sacredness of the sacrament itself by requiring the sacrament be celebrated in that place where the church community normally gathers. A couple that marries in a Catholic church is demonstrating that their faith is an important part of their new life together from the beginning.

26. Why do Catholics receive communion every week when some churches only receive once a month?

The other "churches" you reference are other Christian churches. You hit on the most significant difference between the Catholic Church and other Christian faiths. Remember, all Catholics are Christians but not all Christians are Catholic. Our other Christian brothers, while accepting Jesus Christ, as the Son of God, do not believe that Jesus was speaking literally in John's Gospel when he said, "I am telling you the truth: if you do not eat the flesh of the Son of Man and drink his blood, you will not have life in yourselves. Those who eat my flesh and drink my blood will have eternal life" (Jn 6:53). Our non-Catholic, Christian brothers believe Jesus was speaking figuratively or symbolically and not literally, despite their agreement that Jesus was omniscient (all knowing). Jesus clearly knew the people understood he was speaking literally, and he did not try to change their understanding, rather, he reinforced he was speaking literally. He even predicted many of his own disciples would find his teaching too difficult and would leave him, which they did.

So, here is the difference. As Catholics, The Roman Catholic Church, that is, the Latin Rite Catholic Church, and other Catholic Churches in communion with Rome believe that the Eucharist is the Real Presence of Jesus Christ, body, blood, soul and divinity. The Orthodox Churches and most other Churches of the East do so as well. Anglican [Episcopalian] and other Protestant denominations have interpreted Christ's presence at the celebration of the Lord's Supper or Eucharist to be either only spiritual, or symbolic, or non-existent. Roman Catholics fully believe and accept the gift and the command of Jesus Christ to eat his flesh and drink his blood. Our priests make this gift available, not periodically, not just on Sunday's but every single day of the year.

Jesus reminded the people of his time, and us through the Gospels, that the Jewish peoples' ancestors were given manna in the dessert daily, to meet their physical needs. Jesus said he was giving them a much better food then was given to their ancestors in the dessert, a food that would give them eternal life. The Eucharist is the New Testament fulfillment or superior corollary to manna of the Old Testament. This spiritual life sustaining food is made available to you as a Catholic three hundred sixty-five days a year. Every day of your life you have the privilege and the opportunity to receive Christ.

In the Christian rite, in their equivalent to our Catholic mass, since Christians do not take John's Gospel literally, they do not offer "communion" as in the Catholic rite as Jesus's actual body and blood. Christians offer "communion" as a spiritual "symbol" of his body and blood. My main reason to try to get to daily mass as often as possible, is to take advantage of the greatest gift Christ could possibly have given us, the gift of God himself, for Him to become literally one with us as food that gives us eternal life.

27. Why do Catholics need to drink wine at mass?

Let's be very clear here, while the liquid you drink looks and tastes like wine, once it is consecrated by the priest, it becomes God's blood. The wine, and the bread, are both transubstantiated, changed from mere bread and wine into God's body and blood. Furthermore, you do not have to drink it, you have the privilege to accept God's gift of eternal life by eating his body (the consecrated bread) and drinking his blood (the consecrated wine). We do not always have the privilege of receiving Christ's gift of eternal life under both species (bread and wine), but when we do have such a privilege, and if we are feeling well, we should take advantage of this opportunity. We need to accept this gift, so we can enjoy the bounty of eternal life that Jesus Christ promised us, came to earth to give us, died for us, and made available to us. However, receiving Christ in Holy Eucharist is just as "complete" regardless if you receive one or both forms, the consecrated bread and/or wine which has been "transubstantiated" into God's body and blood. In this daily miracle of the Holy Eucharist, while the bread and wine still look, feel and taste the same as before they were consecrated, their very essence changes into God's body and blood. What a gift we have the privilege to receive every single day of our lives.

28. How can angels not have a gender?

A related question was, "Does everyone see their own guardian angel?"

Angels are neither male nor female. Being pure spirits, they do not possess the bodily traits of gender (Heb 1:13-14, CCC 328, 330). Even so, in Scripture angels appear as males (Gen 19:1-28). The archangel Gabriel is named (Lk: 1:11-20) as are Michael (Rv 12:7) and Raphael (Tb5:4).

The *Catechism of the Catholic Church* confirms the existence of angels stating they are, "spiritual, non-corporeal (means without physical form) beings that Sacred Scripture usually calls 'angels' is a truth of faith. The witness of Scripture is as clear as the unanimity of Tradition. St Augustine says: "Angel" is the name of their office, not of their nature. If you seek the name of their nature, it is "spirit"; if you seek the name of their office, it is angel": from what they are, "spirit" from what they do, "angel". With their whole beings, the angels are servants and messengers of God" (CCC 328-329).

It goes on to say, "As purely spiritual creatures, angels have intelligence and free will: they are personal and immortal creatures, surpassing in perfection all visible creatures, as the splendor of their glory bears witness" (CCC 330). The Catechism of the Catholic Church goes on to cite numerous scriptural references that confirm angels have been present since creation and throughout the history of salvation. Two notable ones include the angel who stayed Abraham's hand from killing his son and the angel who visited Mary. The official definition of an angel according to the Church is: "Angels are intelligent spiritual creatures who glorify God without ceasing and who serve his saving plans for other creatures." According to St. Thomas Aquinas, "The angels work together for the benefit of us all."

But remember, angels are spiritual beings. They have no bodies and therefore no wings either! Even so, angels are often depicted in art as winged in male and female forms. This is so we can better relate to them on a human level and understand something of their power and intelligence.

Angels also have perfect intellects and since they are not human, they are not affected by psychological and emotional passions as we are. Those angels that went against God, understood fully what they were doing and could clearly see the consequences of what their choices would be. Satan and the other angels were created by God and were good (God can only create good). But then Satan and his angels became evil by their own doing (Jn 8:44, Jude 6:7). They chose not to serve God. They desired to exalt themselves above their created condition and make themselves independent of God. As the Catechism of the Catholic Church says, "There is no repentance for the angels after their fall, just as there is no repentance for men after death" (CCC 393).

However, like other angels, Satan can assume an earthly appearance (as the Angel Gabriel did when he appeared to Mary, or as the angel in the tomb following Jesus's resurrection). Saints John Vianney and Stanislaus said they had seen him in the form of a dog. But the most dangerous form the devil assumes is that of an angel of light (2Co 11:14). He appears to be good, but of course, remains evil. Therefore, some medieval art depicts him as a monk with goat horns. The point is that the devil always proposes or tempts us with an evil act as though it is something good, like the forbidden fruit to Adam and Eve.

Since angels are purely spirits, do not have mortal qualities, they never die. However, on the Final Judgment Day, they will be either be permanently banished to hell or they will enjoy eternity in heaven.

I am not personally aware of a documented example of someone seeing his/her own guardian angel but given that angels have appeared to us before by taking a human form, it could very well have happened. Angels are wonderful gifts from God designated to protect and pray for us (Mt 18:10, Ps 91:11-12). They are more faithful and loving than any human could ever conceive of being because they are pure spirits committed to the will of God. As I stated before, Jesus told St. Thomas, "blessed are those who do not see, yet believe". So, while it would really be cool to see my guardian angel, I believe "he" is there for me and I believe is there watching over me!

There is a good book with a collection of angel stories entitled, *Where Angels Walk*, by Joan Wester Anderson. I encourage you to read this as it has some very interesting real-life stories that may help you come to believe or strengthen your belief in angels.

29. Is missing mass on Sunday a venial or mortal sin?

The third commandment requires us to "Keep Holy the Sabbath" which means attending mass each week (Saturday evening or on Sunday) and on Holy Days of Obligation. It is a grave obligation to miss Sunday mass. In fact, it is a mortal sin if you do not attend Sunday mass unless you are sick, infirmed, incapacitated, or if a priest is unavailable (you are vacationing in the jungle or snowbound in an airport) or you are physically unable to get to mass on Sunday. If you cannot drive and it is not practical to walk to mass, you have the obligation to ask your parent or guardian to get you to church. If you ask and they refuse or are themselves not capable of getting you to church, then it is not a sin. Furthermore, once you have missed Sunday mass or a Holy Day mass, you have an obligation to get to Reconciliation, make a good confession, and receive absolution, prior to participating in any other sacrament, including the Holy Eucharist.

Jesus asked his disciples, and was asking us, in the Garden of Gethsemane to pray one hour with him prior to, and in thanks for, his ultimate sacrifice of becoming man, subjecting himself to torture and then to death, to free us from the bonds of original sin. Also, going to mass, just like participating in any other sacrament, provides sanctifying grace or food for our souls. We should take advantage of all the sacraments as much as possible.

So ideally, we do not just go to church every Sunday because we are required to be there. Hopefully, we go because we want to be there, because we appreciate the supreme sacrifice Jesus made for us, and, because we want to set aside time to personally thank him for all the gifts, gifts talents and charisms he has bestowed upon us. Sunday mass provides the opportunity to acknowledge his humility and sacrifice so we could be happy with him in heaven, to pray for others in need, to pray for our own personal needs, and finally, to pray for the grace and strength to accept his will. Through attendance at mass, along with prayer and participating in the other sacraments, we draw closer to God, strengthen are relationship with him, and have more grace and power to resist the temptations of the devil.

30. When people commit suicide, was that God's plan for them? Can they still get to heaven?

A related question was, "Does everything happen for a reason?"

Yet another question was, "If God is good, why is there a Devil?"

The first question really hits home for me as my own best friend and brother-in-law, Paul, who introduced me to his sister Madelyn, who is now my wife, committed suicide in his mid-fifties. All who knew him, including me, could not begin to imagine Paul taking his own life. We just knew there had to be some other explanation. The autopsy revealed that just prior to his suicide, Paul suffered a massive stroke in the side of his brain that controlled rational decisions and emotions. The doctor said that there was no way Paul knew or understood what he was doing. Initially, the coroner refused to do an autopsy as there had been no evidence of foul play so there was no need for an official autopsy. This is standard procedure by the coroner's office where it is clear the person took their own life. The night before Paul was to be buried, his wife had a dream that she should get an autopsy done. The next morning, she canceled the burial ceremony and paid a private physician to conduct a complete autopsy. Had she not paid to have a private autopsy we never would have so clearly known that Paul did not freely commit suicide knowing it was wrong or even knowingly took his own life. The autopsy findings provided a great deal of comfort to his immediate family and all that knew him well.

God does not cause evil to happen but does permit the devil and other natural catastrophes to happen. This is the downside of the fact that he created a beautiful universe and a human race with souls, free wills and superior intellects unlike any of his other creations.

I will paraphrase from Matthew J. Pinto's book, *Did Adam & Eve Have Belly Buttons? And 199 Other Questions from Catholic Teenagers (No. 168).*

We are reminded that only one sin is unforgiveable and that is, a sin against the Holy Spirit, the sin of final impenitence or the failure to repent. Suicide is seriously sinful as human life is a precious gift from God. One who freely chooses to commit suicide with enough reflection and deliberation, knowing it to be seriously sinful, sins mortally.

However, many people who commit suicide may not be doing something they understand to be seriously sinful or may not be acting freely. Severe psychological factors may be involved in the situation. These can diminish the responsibility of the one committing suicide (CCC 2282). Also, we should never underestimate God's saving grace (1Ti 2:3-4). For example, it is said that Jesus appeared to St. Catherine of Siena to tell her that her brother, who committed suicide by jumping from a bridge, had repented before he hit the water. While this story is not doctrine of the Church, it does offer some hope for the families of those who have committed suicide.

Your question on suicide ties in with the related question, "Why does an all-powerful God let evil things happen?"

The Book of Job is a one of my favorite books in the Old Testament. You should know this book is a poetic, didactic book, not necessarily a historical one. That means this book was written to teach, to deliver a specific message to us. Biblical scholars are not even sure who the author of this book was but believe it was written between the seventh and fifth centuries B.C.

Satan, as referenced in this book, is technically not the devil but a title for adversary. So, remember the Book of Job is a story intended to deliver a message. The message is all about how to deal with adversity in our lives and that we need to accept both the good things we are given along with the problems, even very hard ones, as blessings from God. God is giving us these blessings and allowing the bad things to happen as part of His overall redemptive plan.

Randy Alcorn reminds us in his book, *If God is Good,* that God did not create evil, nor does he cause evil, but he does permit evil to exist and he uses evil things and evil people for his ultimate purpose. Some of

Vincent J. Heaton Jr.

the consequences of evil or bad decisions are pain, suffering and death. However, God paid the ultimate sacrifice for all our bad or evil ways by sacrificing his own Son to overcome sin and death. This was part of his plan of "redemptive salvation". Like Job from the Old Testament, or others you may know, like my good friend Jim Harrell who died of the terrible disease of ALS, God calls many of us to carry an extra burden by asking us to accept challenges, so we too can participate in his overall plan of redemptive salvation.

Like other choices we are enabled to make, we can either accept these challenges willingly and gracefully and use them as gifts to help others and give honor and glory to God, or we can turn bitter and cry, "Why me God?" Back in the Old Testament times, some people did not understand this. They felt that anyone who was afflicted with a disease or a handicap, a physical impairment of some kind, that this was given to them as a direct consequence for their own personal sin. They did not understand God's real plan. Pain and suffering are consequences of our human nature, the general weakness of man to resist temptation. And, while God asks some to carry more than their fair share of the pain, he does so with a plan and a purpose. Often, he provides extra blessings of faith, grace and inner strength to help them deal with the burden they have been asked to carry

This is what the Book of Job is all about. Not all respond well and accept the burden and the graces for what they really are. These challenges present opportunities to both save ourselves and to help others achieve salvation by the example we can set, and by willingly accepting these challenges, using them for God's greater honor and glory. Fr. James Spitzer's seventh module in his *Credible Catholic* series does a wonderful job of covering this whole question of why and how and all powerful and all loving God could permit pain and suffering to occur.

Remember the gospel about the rich man and the beggar Lazarus? The rich man ignored Lazarus's plea for food and drink. When the rich man died and went to hell and found out it was too late for him and that Lazarus could not cross from heaven to hell to give him a sip of water, he asked God to send Lazarus back to earth to warn his brothers. God responded by saying if they do not listen to the prophets or Sacred Scripture they will not listen to someone who has returned from the dead (this is also a subtle reference to the son of God, becoming incarnate, allowing us to torture and crucify him and then rising from the dead to open the gates of heaven, and to us that we should listen to what Jesus said to all of us!).

God gives us all we need to make good decisions and to bear the crosses he challenges us with. They key is that we also have the power to make bad decisions or to refuse to accept the crosses he burdens us with (such as by getting mad at God when a loved one dies, or when a storm damages an entire town, or more personally, when something bad or difficult to accept happens to us).

31. What is the difference between God, Christ and Jesus?

I understand how all these titles can be confusing!

Let me start with "Christ". Christ is the New Testament Greek equivalent to the Old Testament Hebrew word "Messiah", both of which mean "anointed". So, both titles refer to the savior promised in the Old Testament and the fulfillment of the promise in the form of Jesus as that "Messiah" or "Christ". Andrew first found his own brother Simon, and said to him, "We have found the Messiah," which is, being interpreted, the Christ. And he brought him to Jesus" (Jn 1: 41-42).

So, Jesus and Christ are one in the same. Furthermore, we know Jesus is the third person in the Trinity, also known as God the Son. As Catholics we believe there are three persons in one God. God the Father and the Holy Spirit are the other two persons.

Trying to explain the Trinity is heady stuff and I don't claim to be any better, (not even close) to St. Patrick who helped simplify our grasp of this very faith based dogmatic principle. He used the three-leafed clover to explain. Let me take a slightly different but parallel tact. We as human beings have a hard time understanding things that are divine in nature. The fact they are divine in nature and not human or physical in nature, implies we are going to have a hard time. We can begin to understand divine qualities or matters of faith if we can bring them down to our level, to give them natures or properties we can relate to.

The Trinity, or three persons in one God, shows God has multiple aspects that are "revealed" to us as three different persons even though their divine natures are all one, or part of the same "One". Fr. Hardon's, *The Question and Answer Catholic Catechism* (a great book to have in your house), explains that, "the three Persons are distinct from one another in that the Father has no origin, the Son is begotten or comes from the Father alone; and the Holy Spirit proceeds or comes from the Father and the Son" (Jn 16:28; 15:26). Yet, though truly distinct, the three Persons have one and the same divine nature. To confirm that there are three persons in one God, read Matthew's Gospel where Jesus tells his apostles, "make disciples of all nations; baptize them in the name of the Father, the Son and the Holy Spirit" (Mt 28:19). So, I believe the point of the Trinity is to help us better know the full nature(s) of God, to better know him as he fully is but within the limits of our human comprehension to know all sides of him.

32. Since Mary was born without original sin, isn't she really a divine being because it says (in the Bible) all men were born with sin?

You are mixing two dogmatic topics in your question. One is how Mary could have been born without original sin when the Bible clearly states "all" men are born with original sin. The second is a more philosophical challenge to our Catholic belief in that we as Catholics are asked, "how could Mary, a mere mortal, give birth to a divine being?" The argument is that either Mary did not give birth to the Son of God, or if she did, she too would have to be a god.

In a way, this last question, was the same question Mary asked of the angel Gabriel when he came as God's messenger to ask Mary if she would be the

Mother of the Son of God, "Then the angel said to her, "Do not be afraid, Mary, you have found favor with God. Behold you will conceive in your womb and bear a son, and you shall name him Jesus. He will be great and be called son of the Most-High, and the Lord God will give him the throne of David his father, and he will rule over the house of Jacob forever, and of his kingdom there will be no end." But Mary said to the angel, "How shall this be since I have no relations with a man?" And the angel said to her in reply, "The Holy Spirit will come upon you, and the power of the Most-High will overshadow you. Therefore, the child to be born will be called holy, the Son of God" *(Luke 1:30-35).*

So, Mary was conceived by the Holy Spirit, which while difficult to comprehend, makes sense on another level. We may have trouble grasping the fact that God, (by the way, the same God that created our entire complex and beautiful universe) could miraculously cause a woman to be able to conceive a child through the intervention of the Holy Spirit. However, it does help explain how Mary could give birth to Jesus who was both wholly God and wholly man. Mary contributed to his human nature and the Holy Spirit, to his divine nature. For this reason, we refer to the Holy Spirit as Mary's spouse. Joseph is Jesus's stepfather.

The analogous aspect of this special birth to all other human births is that our parents are the cause or determinant of our human natures, that is, of all our physical characteristics and it is the Holy Spirit, the third person in the Trinity, that is the determinant or cause of our spiritual natures, our souls. When the Church says we are born "in the image and likeness of Christ", the Church is referring to this gift of spiritual life and the initial sanctifying grace we are born with. We are "God-like" only in so far as we have souls, souls that live eternally, that do not die when our mortal bodies die.

This eternal quality or attribute can only come from a supreme being, not a human being. We know this gift of an eternal spiritual life or soul is unique to us as human beings. No other creature, plant or thing has such a soul. Nor do they have "free wills" and "intellects" which are also special unique gifts from God to all human beings. There is scientific evidence for the existence of our souls. I encourage you to check out Fr. Robert Spitzer's *Credible Catholic* modules (specifically module one) for details on this.

So, if this concept of Mary conceiving by the Holy Spirit "overshadowing her" seems difficult, remember what Jesus said to his disciples in John's Gospel (*The Bread of Life Discourse*, Jn 6) when he knew they had trouble grasping that they must eat his body and drink his blood to have everlasting life? He asked them, "Does this shock you? What if you were to see the Son of Man ascending to where he was before (i.e. heaven)?" (*Jn 6:61*). In other words, Jesus was saying to them if you think this concept is hard to grasp, stick around a while with me guys because there is more shock and awe yet to come! So, it is hard for us to accept that Mary could have become pregnant without "knowing man", but if we accept the fact that there must be a God, and that God created the universe, and that Jesus is the Son of God, then it should not be too hard to accept the concept of the virgin birth.

Which by the way, many confuse the virgin birth with the Immaculate Conception (feast day we celebrate on December 8th). Of course, you now know we celebrate Mary being born without original sin on the feast of the Immaculate Conception. This feast, and the feast of the Assumption are also difficult concepts to accept but again are very logical when you think about them in a broader theological context.

Regarding the apparent contradiction with the Bible regarding Mary being born without original sin. As I stated in class, this question underscores the flaws in a very fundamentalist view of the protestant doctrine of *sola scriptura* which is the view that if it is written in the Bible we will accept it as written and if it is not specifically written in the Bible we will not accept it as part of our faith doctrine.

I have covered this point in response to other questions but in short, while we as Catholics believe the Bible is one-hundred percent true in terms of the message God intended, not all the specific points in the Bible are to be taken one hundred percent literally.

We can prove this by reminding our protestant friends that Adam and Eve were born without Original Sin just like Mary (although they will argue this point applies to post Adam and Eve, persons…but then they still are not taking the written word totally literally). Furthermore, Jesus who they agree was both fully God and fully man, was also not born with Original Sin.

I also ask protestants who hold firmly to the sola scriptura doctrine if they believe in the Trinity, three persons in one God. So far, all have responded in the affirmative. I then ask them to show me where in the Bible it references the Trinity, especially with the specific clarification that all three persons are separate natures but all part of one God. They will never find it because it is not there. In short, this helps underscore why Jesus left us a Church structure/hierarchy and the Magisterium, the teaching body of the Church. We rely on the Church/Magisterium to help us apply Sacred Scripture to our ever-changing lives'/world.

33. How was Mary Assumed into Heaven?

So, there are a few ways to interpret this question. I will cover what I believe to be central to what you are asking but will cover related points in my all-encompassing style!

On a literal level, the Assumption of Mary (or the Assumption of the Virgin) is the doctrine which teaches that shortly after the mother of Jesus died, she was resurrected, glorified, and taken bodily to heaven. The word assumption is taken from a Latin word meaning "to take up." This in contrast to Jesus's ascension (to rise up) into heaven. Jesus as our omnipotent (all powerful) God (divine being) had the ability to rise on his own power whereas Mary, a human being, needed God's omnipotent power to cause her to rise or be assumed into heaven. The "Assumption of Mary" is taught by the Roman Catholic Church and, to a lesser degree, by the Eastern Orthodox Church.

On a historical level, the doctrine of the Assumption of Mary had its beginnings in the Byzantine Empire around the 6th Century. An annual feast honoring Mary gradually grew into a commemoration of Mary's death called the Feast of Dormition ("falling asleep"). As the practice spread to the West, an emphasis was placed on Mary's resurrection, and the glorification of Mary's body as well as her soul, and the name of the feast was thereby changed to the Assumption. It is still observed on August 15, as it was in the Middle Ages. The Assumption of Mary was made an official dogma of the Roman Catholic Church in 1950 by Pope Pius XII. This dogmatic position, along with the official dogma regarding the Immaculate Conception (Mary's birth without the stain of original sin) are the only two official "ex cathedra" (from the throne) infallible statements by any pope in the entire history of the Church. Please note there have been many other infallible statements or proclamations by Roman Catholic popes but none as official as these ex cathedra statements.

But why would Jesus assume Mary into heaven? Does this make sense? Is there a scriptural basis for this? And is there any biblical precedent? The answers are yes, on a theological level; and no there is no direct scriptural reference to Mary's assumption. However, there are several indirect references to her glorious assumption, just like the trinity doctrine; and, yes, the Bible does record God "assuming" both Enoch and Elijah into heaven. Therefore, the doctrine of Mary's assumption has both a scriptural history or precedent and a logical basis when one considers Mary's total role or calling. As does the other ex-cathedra papal doctrine of Mary's Immaculate Conception.

On a theological level, we must remember the New Testament, which essentially begins with the birth of Jesus, is the fulfillment of Old Testament prophecies. Jesus fulfilled over three-hundred different Old Testament prophecies, twenty-nine of these in a single day! There are numerous examples of people and things in the New Testament that have direct counterparts in the Old Testament, but the New Testament person or object is always superior to its Old Testament counterpart. Eve, who is Mary's Old Testament counterpart, was, like Mary, also born without sin.

However, Mary is superior to Eve for Mary never committed sin, while of course Eve committed the first or Original Sin.

The Old Testament Ark of the Covenant, which is described in Exodus, was a special vessel designed by Yahweh/God that contained the Ten Commandments, Aaron's rod, manna, and finally Sacred Scripture, scrolls or "The Word", is the inferior counterpart object to Mary. The Ark was seen only by Levite priests and was never touched directly, even by the priests, as they used cloth to avoid direct contact. When the Israelites travelled from place to place in their quest for the Holy Land, they used long rods that were inserted through rings to avoid direct contact. This was all because this sacred vessel contained God's commandments and his Word.

Mary, and specifically her womb is the New Testament superior to the Ark as Mary was to bear Jesus, the Word incarnate (made flesh) in her womb. So, it follows that she would be born without blemish, perfect, without sin (Immaculately Conceived) so her womb would be the perfect vessel to deliver Jesus). It further follows that Mary would remain perfect (with the help of God's special sanctifying graces) throughout her life. It then further follows that God, having known Mary would agree to be the Mother of Jesus and would remain sinless, that he would not let that perfect body turn to dust upon her death.

You must remember that sacred scripture and Jesus promised us that on the Final Judgment Day, our souls will all be reunited with our glorified bodies (our bodies will never need food, get sick or cold, etc.) and spend eternity either in heaven or in hell. God appropriately granted this state to Mary ahead of time to keep her "perfected in grace" which is the Greek translation of the angel Gabriel's greeting to Mary. In Greek, Luke's Gospel reads, *"chaire kecharitomene"*, or "Hail, one perfected in grace" which indicates a unique abundance of a god-like state which finds its explanation only in the Immaculate Conception.

I encourage you to read up on these doctrines in the *Catechism of the Catholic Church*. But when viewed in the whole context of Mary's role as the mother of Christ, I trust you can begin to see the logic behind both the Assumption and the Immaculate Conception of Mary. God certainly had the power to do this since he initially made our bodies perfect and promised to restore us to this glorified state on the Final Day. Christians believe this last part, so I think it is easier to defend these uniquely Catholic doctrines if you start from the Final Judgment Day premise!

34. How do men get chosen /put into high positions in the Church (like Bishop, Cardinal, Pope)?

This process has evolved over the history of the Catholic Church which now spans 266 Pope's since Jesus effectively named Peter (formerly known as Simon) the first Pope culminating with our current Pope Frances. So, starting at the top, the Pope is now elected by the "College of Cardinals". Popes are elected by the College of Cardinals meeting in Conclave when the Apostolic See, the Papacy, falls vacant.

Pope Paul VI significantly changed the rules for conclaves in 1975 when he promulgated the Apostolic Constitution *Romano Pontifico Eligendo*. He excluded all cardinals eighty years old or over from the conclave and made provisions to prevent any bugging of the Sistine Chapel.

It was according to these rules that Albano Luciano, Patriarch of Venice, was elected Pope John Paul I and then a little over a month later, Karol Wojtyla, Cardinal Archbishop of Krakow, was elected Pope John Paul II. Pope John Paul II himself promulgated a whole new set of rules in 1996 in the Apostolic Constitution.

He has not departed radically from the traditional structure. But he has made some significant changes:

- if no Cardinal has been elected by two-thirds majority after a certain number of ballots, the cardinals may agree by absolute majority (half + one) to elect the Pope by an absolute majority instead of a two-thirds majority

- rather than stay in uncomfortable, makeshift quarters in the Papal Palace, the Cardinals will stay in the *Domus Sanctae Marthae*, hotel-style accommodation in Vatican City
- the only remaining method of electing the Pope is by scrutiny, ie, silent ballot -- the methods of election by acclamation and by committee have been excluded (but were rarely used)
- the older Cardinals are still unable to enter the conclave, but they are invited to take an active role in the preparatory meetings
- the rules on secrecy are tougher

The maximum number of Cardinal Electors allowed at any one time is one hundred-twenty. The pope cannot raise more than one hundred twenty men under eighty to the Cardinalate at any one time. (Of course, being pope, he can also dispense himself with compliance with that rule! On the last two occasions, the pope named new cardinals soon after the number of electors fell below one hundred twenty. There were as high as one hundred thirty-five electors at some stages.) As in April 2005, there are one hundred seventeen Cardinals eligible to vote in Conclave. (Only 115 of them entered the 2005 Conclave, as two of them were too ill to travel to Rome for the Conclave.)

The Conclave

The Cardinals must take an oath when they first enter the Conclave that they will follow the rules set down by the Pope and that they will maintain absolute secrecy about the voting and deliberations. The penalty for disclosing anything about the conclave that must be kept secret is automatic excommunication.

The Cardinals all take seats around the wall of the Sistine Chapel and take a ballot paper on which is written "Eligo in summum pontificem" -- "I elect as supreme pontiff...". They then write a name on it, fold it, and then proceed one by one to approach the altar, where a chalice stands with a paten on it. They hold up their ballot high to show that they have voted, then place it on the paten, and then slide it into the chalice. The votes are then counted by the Cardinal Camerlengo and his three assistants.

Each assistant reads the name, reads the name aloud, writes it down on a tally sheet and then passes it to the next assistant. The third assistant runs a needle and thread through the center of each ballot to join them all together. The ballots are then burned, as well as all notes made. If a new Pope has been elected, the papers are burned with chemicals (it used to be wet straw) to give white smoke. Otherwise, they give off black smoke, so that the waiting crowds, and the world, know whether their new Holy Father will soon emerge from the Sistine Chapel. On April 6, 2005, it was announced that, in addition to the white smoke, the bells of St Peter's Basilica will be rung to signal the election of the new Pope. This will avoid any doubt about whether the smoke is white or black.

Until the conclaves of 1978, each Cardinal was provided a throne and a table and a canopy (or *baldachino*) over their heads. Pope Paul VI abolished the practice because, with the internationalization of the College of Cardinals, there was simply no room anymore. Whereas there were only eighty electors before then, the number had risen to one hundred twenty. The thrones used to be arranged in two rows, along the wall facing each other. The canopies and thrones symbolized that, during the *sede vacante* when there is no Pope, the Cardinals all share responsibility for the governance of the Church. To further this symbolism, once the new Pope was elected and announced the name he would use, the other Cardinals would pull on a cord and the canopy would collapse, leaving just the new Pope with his canopy aloft.

To be elected Pope, one Cardinal must receive at least two-thirds of the votes. Except that, under the new rules established by Pope John Paul II, if a certain number of ballots have taken place without any Cardinal being elected Pope, then the Cardinals may then elect by simple majority. This is an important change and may well be the most important change made. In the past, it has often been the case that a particular candidate has had solid majority support but cannot garner the required two-thirds majority, e.g., because he is too conservative to satisfy the more moderate Cardinals. Therefore, a compromise candidate is chosen, either an old Pope who will die soon and not do much until the next conclave (which is what was intended with John XXIII!) or someone not so hardline wins support. The difference now will be that if, in the early ballots, one candidate has strong majority support, there is less incentive for that majority to compromise with the cardinals who are against their candidate and they simply need to sit out 30 ballots to elect their man. This may well see much more "hardline" Popes being elected. There will also be far less incentive for the Cardinals to finish quickly as in the past. After such a long papacy, they may need time to arrive at a strong consensus on what type of papacy the Church now needs. They will also be staying in comfortable lodgings, rather than sleeping in foldaway cots in hallways and offices in the Sistine Chapel. On the other hand, the Cardinals will be reluctant for it to appear as if they are deeply divided, so there will still be an overriding desire to have a quick conclave. (No conclave in the last two hundred years has lasted more than five days.)

The Cardinals vote on the afternoon of the first day, then twice each morning and twice each afternoon. If they have not elected someone within the first three votes, then they may devote up to a day to prayer and discussion before resuming. They may do the same every seven unsuccessful votes after that.

The Cardinals are not permitted any contact with the outside world: no mobile phones, no newspapers or television, no messages or letters or signals to observers. There will be regular sweeps of all relevant areas for listening devices. The Cardinals will for the first time be able to move freely within Vatican City (i.e., taking a walk in the Vatican Gardens, or walking from the Domus Sanctae Marthae to the Sistine Chapel). Workers in Vatican City continue to go about their business during the Conclave. If they run into a Cardinal, they are forbidden from speaking to him.

The Pope then has the authority to promote priests to become either bishops or cardinals. Cardinals are more senior bishops or bishops with larger dioceses. The pope requests input from other bishops/cardinals and his own advisors on candidates for the episcopacy or the cardinalate.

35. Even though not going to Church on Sunday is a mortal sin if I go to the Sacrament of Reconciliation will I have a clean slate?

I will give you a qualified yes. Making a good confession is the key which includes making a real commitment to change, to be better and to avoid the occasion of sin. So, while we are human and will make bad choices, you cannot simply use confession intentionally like a revolving door of sin/confess/sin/confess, etc. You cannot go into confession asking for forgiveness without also making a commitment to change to amend your life, or in this case, to go regularly to mass on Sunday's and Holy Days of Obligation. You cannot go in simply saying I am sorry while fully intending to go right on missing mass. That said, we are all human and given our weak mortal natures, we will succumb to temptation and will continue to sin, often repeating the same sins over and over again.

One of the tactics of the devil is to get us to believe that we can never change and that our prior commitment to "amend or lives" was not heartfelt. He tries to get us to "give-up" and quit trying, quit going to Reconciliation. Even worse, he will try to get us to rationalize that one or more of these "more frequent" sins are not sinful. Everyone does this, so it must not be wrong. Or, God "made me this way", so why try to change. This is often the case with the sin of pornography.

I would also add to this question, why *should* we *go* to confession? Jesus established, as part of his becoming man and fulfilling the Old Testament prophecies, seven sacraments as a means for us to receive sanctifying grace. Sanctifying grace gives us the strength to resist temptation and acts like food for our souls, our spiritual life. Remember Jesus abolished all but nine of the six hundred thirteen original Laws of the Torah and established a "new law". Jesus established the Sacrament of Penance or Reconciliation on Easter Sunday night when he appeared to his disciples (Jn 20:19-23) and said "Peace be with you. As the Father sent me, so I am sending you." Then he breathed on them and said, receive the Holy Spirit. For those sins you shall forgive they are forgiven and those sins you retain, they are retained." To receive absolution from sin we must make a good confession, which includes three parts, contrition (being truly sorry), confession (verbally stating your sins, your sorrow and your intent to change), and satisfaction (restitution or penance, something to help you atone or make up for your sin).

Fr. Hardon's, *The Question and Answer Catholic Catechism*, explains that Jesus gave the apostles, the first priests, the power to both forgive and to hold sins fast (and the power required for all the sacraments). This underscores Jesus's intent for us to humble ourselves and to show we truly are contrite or sorry by verbally expressing our sins to a priest. The priest can withhold absolution if he does not feel the person is truly sorry or truly committed to change. Some may ask, "then why does the Church allow general confessions and general absolution?" General absolutions are only supposed to be granted under extreme conditions (battlefield) and the absolution is only valid, if all other normal confession terms are met. These absolutions are granted with the understanding that when you can, you will go and make a personal confession as soon as you can (particularly crucial for absolution of mortal sin). So personal confessions are an important means of receiving absolution and Jesus's sanctifying grace.

36. Why was Mary chosen to be born without sin? Why wasn't it someone else?

It might very well have been someone other than Mary but if you consider the qualifications, there probably would not have been many potential candidates, but this does not address your question. So, your question really is why was Mary born without sin at all and then, why her? The answer to that lies in the fact that she was asked to be, and she agreed, to be the Mother of Jesus, God the Son. The Catholic Church believes Mary was born without Original Sin (we celebrate her Immaculate Conception on December 8th) and that her immaculate nature makes sense given her role as the mother of Jesus. Read on.

So, it really was a two-way choice, God had to choose Mary and Mary had to say yes. Like all of us, God makes grace available to us to do great things, greater than we could ever imagine and certainly greater than we could ever do without this grace. However, he made us unique, he made us superior to all other life forms for he gave us free wills to accept or reject his gifts of grace, his teachings, his laws and his will for us. We can accept or reject him in small ways or in big ways, we can accept him all the time, none of the time, some of the time, or most of the time, and everything in between.

I don't believe God randomly chose Mary to be Jesus's mother. The mother of Jesus had to be a very special woman who was worthy of being the mother of our Lord and had to remain so throughout her life. God is omniscient, all knowing. He knew before Mary was born what decisions she would make and how she would live her life.

God gave all of us free wills, so we could make our own choices and choose to good over evil. This is not one decision but a steady stream of small, everyday decisions. God knew what her decisions would be from the very largest, most important decision (i.e. how she would respond to his call through the Angel Gabriel) right down to the least significant decision. For Mary, the hard decision was not so much to agree to give birth to Jesus (although to do so as an unwed mother back then was no easy decision, actually it was huge for she knew she could be stoned to death as an unwed but pregnant woman) but rather, to continually choose to do the right thing, to avoid the devil's temptations not to sin…. every single day of her life. She remained strong and consistently resisted the devils attempts.

God knew she would be strong and remain sinless and he wanted the perfect "vessel", the perfect Ark of the Covenant, for the "Word to become flesh or incarnate and dwell among us", a New Testament superior to Eve, a woman that could be a good role model for all mankind. Mary's womb is the New Testament equivalent to the Ark of the Covenant. The Ark held Sacred Scripture which is known as the "Word of God". The Ark was never physically touched by non-priestly hands and even then, the priests used cloths to open or hold the Ark. When they travelled with the

Ark, men carried it by slipping long rods through loops along the sides of the Ark so that it could be kept pristine and "untouched". So, therefore it makes sense that Mary, as the mother of Jesus, who is the "Word Made Flesh" would be superior to the Ark and in human form would be pristine or immaculate in all ways and untouched or a virgin.

Jesus knew Mary would respond positively to his call for her vocation in life through the request delivered by the Angel Gabriel. For all these very good reasons he chose Mary to be Jesus's mother. As such, he enabled Mary to be conceived immaculately, that is, to be born without original sin and then rewarded her by not only having her be Jesus's mother but by also assuming her into heaven upon her death, in both body and soul. He could not let this special woman/vessel be defiled by having her body whither and turn to dust, so she was assumed, body and soul into heaven. We celebrate the feast of the Assumption on August fifteenth.

Now, I also believe, God blessed Mary with special graces, strength and helped her to remain sinless throughout her mortal life. Could God have selected other women that could have remained sinless and thus qualify to have been born without sin? Sure, God was also omnipotent, all powerful, a supreme being. He can do anything. However, he only needed one, albeit one very special woman, to be his mother.

Due to God's omniscient, all knowing power, he knew Mary would not only say yes to his vocation for her through the Angel Gabriel regarding accepting the role of Mother of Christ, but that she would consistently and fully accept all his gifts of grace and totally resist the temptations of the devil and never commit a sin.

37. What determines if you go to heaven or to hell? And, another question was, "What do you have to do to get to heaven"?

Thankfully it is our most loving and forgiving God whom we face on the Final Judgement Day and while he makes the final call on who gets to heaven and who is banished for eternity in hell, it is how we live our lives here on earth and the choices we make that determines our fate. God does not really send us to hell, those that go to hell, go there of their own accord, they decide to reject God directly or indirectly. Regardless of the decisions we make God will always love us but that does not mean there will not be consequences of our actions. We decide to accept or to reject Jesus and his teachings. God gave us the law to follow, the Ten Commandments. Then, when God sent his only Son to become man and overcome sin and death by his crucifixion and resurrection, he built on these Ten Commandments. He gave us an "eleventh" commandment, the Great Commandment and the Beatitudes. Jesus expanded his expectations of us from Old Testament times when he gave Moses the Ten Commandments (these were mainly the list of things we should NOT do). He taught that it was also important TO DO certain things, to use our time, treasure and talents (which are all gifts from God that he "loans" to us) for the good of others.

So, when you go to the Sacrament of Reconciliation you should not only consider the sins you committed or the commandments you broke but also the things you failed to do (sins of omission). These include: failing to stick up for kids in school who are getting bullied or talked down to; willingly helping your parents or neighbors, or others in need; giving your best in school, etc. As you grow older the expectations Jesus has for you will grow as well. Helping your neighbor and treating people as Jesus taught us to will take on a greater dimension. Thankfully we have a most loving and merciful God who forgives us, repeatedly, despite our frequent transgressions. Fortunately, God does not judge us like men judge their fellow man (which is why I am glad a jury of our peers does not decide if we go to heaven or hell). Jesus forgave even those men that subjected him to the worst form of death possible at his time and to an in-humanly cruel and excessive beating prior to this death…. right as they were beating and crucifying him! I would say that is one forgiving God.

God does have high expectations of us, but he is also highly forgiving and eternally merciful. Consider the rich young man who confronted Jesus and said, "All of these I have observed (referring to the commandments). What do I still lack" (Mt 19:20)? To the rich man's chagrin, Jesus responded by saying, "If you wish to be perfect, go, sell what you have and give to the poor and you will have treasure in heaven. Then, come follow me" (Mt19:21). This was too much for the man and he went away disappointed. God does have high expectations but all he wants is for us to use the gifts, resources and talents he gave us to his greater honor and glory, to our fullest possible extent.

I do not believe Jesus intended us to take this parable one hundred percent literally and sell all our possessions. The rich man was looking for a "guaranteed path to heaven and Jesus was saying, "do what I do". I believe his message is we should NEVER value or treat anything more important than God. This includes our parents, our spouse, our children, money, food, power, fame, etc.

The Great Commandment says, "You shall love the Lord your God, with all your heart, with all your being, with all your strength, and with all your mind, and love your neighbor as yourself" (Lk 10:27). Also, remember that Jesus even further expanded on the Great Commandment by giving us an even newer commandment, "A new command I give you: Love one another. As I have loved you, so you must love one another" (Jn 13:34). Think about this in relationship to all Ten Commandments. If we follow the Great Commandment to the fullest, we will by default, follow all Ten Commandments. That said, we are by nature, sinful and will turn against God and his teachings, his laws and his commandments, repeatedly.

However, Jesus gave us the Sacrament of Reconciliation to humble ourselves, to repent and to be forgiven of our sins. This and other sacraments are a source of sanctifying grace. This grace gives us strength to help make better decisions and to resist the devil's attacks that are designed to lead us away from Christ. God knows that despite our good intentions, we will stumble again, and make more bad choices, yet he stands ready to forgive us repeatedly. While this does not give us license to wantonly sin as victims of our natural weak human natures, it does provide solace that God will always keep the door open for those that want to take advantage of his mercy.

38. What are the minimum requirements for two Catholics to marry?

So first to clarify, the Catholic Church will marry a couple even if one of the two is not Catholic. Before the Second Vatican Council, if a Catholic planned on marrying someone, who was not Catholic, the Church strongly encouraged the non-Catholic to convert prior to the wedding. If the person was not open to conversion, then he/she was required to agree to raise their children in the Catholic faith. However, the Catholic Church has much more tolerant policies towards mixed religion marriages and no longer pushes for the non-Catholic to convert and they are not required to take an active role in raising children in the Catholic faith.

For a valid Catholic marriage, the wedding must be officiated by a Catholic priest and several components need to be present. These components fall into three major categories: capacity, consent and form. Let me explain at a very high or general level what these component areas entail.

Capacity – The person(s) must have the ability to get married which means, they can't already be married (can't be divorced from a prior marriage and having multiple spouses is unacceptable), must be old enough and each party must understand what he/she is committing to.

Consent – Consent is the act of freely and fully giving oneself to the other. So, one can't simply be "trying marriage on to see if it works for them". This is also where each person must agree to the "gift" of children in their marriage commit to be responsible parents for each child born of the marriage. Both individuals must be of sound mind.

Form – Form is how the marriage is contracted. The marriage must be officiated by a priest or deacon and witnessed by two parties for it to be valid. In most cases the ceremony must take place in a Catholic Church.

So, if a priest/deacon interviews the engaged couple and finds they do not meet the basic requirements of these three component areas he cannot marry them. There are other requirements like attending a pre-Cana conference and other related details but the above represent the key requirements.

39. What do protestants mean by "being saved"?

Many non-Catholic, Christian faith denominations, believe that once a person formally accepts Jesus as their personal Lord and Savior, they will be assured of enjoying eternal happiness with God in heaven. Under a strict interpretation of this protestant doctrine of *sola fide,* by faith alone, they believe that it does not really matter how you live your life or what specific religious beliefs and practices you follow in your life. Once you accept Jesus as your Lord and Savior you will get to heaven or you will be "saved". It might loosely be likened to becoming a "made man" in the Italian mafia, once "made" you are protected against hits from your brother mafioso. Ok, I apologize as I stretch the analogy a bit, but you get my drift.

Many Christians believe we Catholics think that we can "make up for our sins" by doing kind acts to "earn" our way into heaven. This is not what the Catholic Church believes or teaches. Catholics believe as the apostle James said, "faith without works is dead" (Jas 2:26). Works is synonymous with kind acts or things we do to live our faith. Catholics do not believe we can ever make up for our sinful ways but if we are to be forgiven and be happy with God in heaven, we must show remorse and ask God's forgiveness and continue to try to avoid sin. Catholics also believe they have an obligation to use the gifts God gave each one of us for his greater honor and glory.

If you are ever asked "Are you saved?" or, "Have you accepted Jesus as your personal Lord and Savior?", you should reply firmly and positively, "yes, I have accepted Jesus as my Lord and Savior and I have a confident assurance that I will enjoy eternal life with him in heaven"…confident but not guaranteed. As to accepting Jesus, you were baptized a Catholic and hopefully raised as a practicing Catholic since your baptism. By living your faith each day, you are affirming your belief in Jesus as your Lord and Savior. In the Sacrament of Confirmation, the final step to full initiation into the Catholic Church, you formally re-affirm your belief in Jesus and your commitment to live a good Catholic life. As to whether you are saved or not, I always respond, "I have confident assurance" I will enjoy eternal life with God in heaven if I continue to live a good Catholic life, seek forgiveness for my sinful ways regularly through the Sacrament of Reconciliation and remain committed to amending my sinful ways.

40. Why do Catholics accept the Pope as the authoritative head of the Church?

Read Chapter 16 of Matthew's Gospel for just one scriptural proof point that Jesus established Peter as the first head of his Church on earth. Also read Chapter 21 of John's Gospel where Jesus, after he rose from the dead, reaffirms Peter as the head of the Church, even though Peter denied Jesus three times during his trial before he was condemned to death.

Remember my analogy of Jesus establishing a hierarchy with the Pope as the head and disciples (bishops) as his aides, as the teaching body or magisterium of his Church to that of our founding fathers establishing an order through the constitution with amendments and a three-branch system of government. It took great foresight for our founding fathers to recognize that times would change and that the government structure they established would need to be able to flex to those changing times so it could remain strong and dynamic without changing its core principles and democratic form of government and survive for generations to come. Doesn't it make sense that an all-knowing God would have at least as much foresight as our founding fathers? Jesus knew, that over time, his Church on earth would need help and guidance and structure to remain strong and resilient to the devil's attacks. Why would God the Son, become man, save us from the pains of original sin by letting men beat and crucify him, only to rise from the dead and ascend into heaven, without leaving some structure behind?? This just does not make sense. He knew we would need help and guidance to apply his teachings (Sacred Scripture) to this ever-changing world. This is what Jesus intended the Pope to do with the help of his bishops, priests and key lay persons (the magisterium).

41. What is the sacrament for the sick called and what is its purpose?

The sacrament you are referring to is called *Anointing of the Sick* but it was once called *Extreme Unction*. The reason for the name change coincided with the Church's practice regarding this sacrament. Extreme Unction was only provided to those very near or at the point of death where now, Anointing of the Sick is intended for the gravely ill and for the very advanced in age. The rite itself has also changed to better suit today's medical/hospital environment (won't go into the details on this but you can read up on it if you like)

So, what you are really asking is what the spiritual effects are of this sacrament. Fr. John Hardon, S.J. addresses this question in his book, *The Question and Answer Catholic Catechism (pages 297-303)*. This is another great resource that should be in every Catholic home. Fr. Hardon tells us, "The spiritual effects of anointing are: forgiveness of the guilt of unremitted sin, even grave sin, for which the person had at least imperfect sorrow; remission of the temporal punishment (this is restitution or a sort of making up for your sin, your penance) still due for remitted (forgiven) sin, to such a degree that the expiation (amends or penance) can be complete; supernatural patience to bear with the sufferings of one's illness; extraordinary confidence in God's mercy, which a person certainly needs when he faces eternity; and special infusion of courage to resist the temptation of the devil".

Since this sacrament remits all previous sin and the related unsatisfied temporal punishment, provided that at some time the person had, in faith, been truly sorry for his sins, the recipient is clean, and his soul goes to heaven. Immediately following death, we receive a "particular judgment" that determines our eternal fate, heaven or hell. If our eternal fate is heaven, but our souls carry the stain of sin, we spend time "in Purgatory" (think of purgatory not as a place but a process) to get cleansed of this sin. Then, at the end of time, at the time of the Final Judgment, our souls will be reunited with our resurrected bodies (they will never die again, get sick, feel pain, get hungry, etc.) and we will either enjoy life in heaven or on the New Earth (for heaven may be just like being on a "Garden of Eden" like earth with plants, animals but with no pain and suffering, or we may end up in hell.

42. Why do Catholics have to go to Reconciliation with a priest, why can't we simply talk to God directly as we do in prayer?

Jesus told us that just praying directly to God for forgiveness is not enough. He told us we must go to the Sacrament of Reconciliation to be forgiven and that we must pay restitution or fulfill some form of temporal punishment. Furthermore, as Catholics we cannot participate in other sacraments, like Holy Eucharist, if we have mortal or grave sins on our souls. Even if we only have committed venial, less serious sins, it is always a good idea before you receive the Sacrament of Holy Eucharist to pray to God expressing sorrow for any sins you may have committed and to ask for forgiveness, if you cannot get to Reconciliation beforehand. Please note, if you have missed Sunday mass (unless you were seriously ill, or could not physically get to mass), this is a mortal sin and you are not allowed to receive the Holy Eucharist until you have gone to confession. Unfortunately, not all Catholics even know this is Catholic Church teaching let alone live their lives accordingly.

You must know something is wrong before it can be a sin, but now you know!! By now you also know I do not believe in short answers, so let me finish answering your good question. I would also add to your question, why *should* we go to confession? So, what you are asking is, "why can't I just talk to God directly, why do I have to go through a third party, a priest?" The answer is that Jesus established, as part of becoming man and fulfilling the Old Testament prophecies, seven sacraments as a means for us to receive sanctifying grace. Jesus established the Sacrament of Penance or Reconciliation on Easter Sunday night when he appeared to his disciples and said "Receive the Holy Spirit. Whose sins you forgive are forgiven them, and whose sins you retain are retained" (Jn 20:22-23).

To receive absolution from sin we must make a good confession, which includes three parts: contrition (being truly sorry); confession (verbally stating your sins, your sorrow and your intent to change); and, satisfaction (restitution or penance, something to help you atone or make up for your sin). Fr. Hardon's, *The Question and Answer Catholic Catechism*, directly addresses your question. He explains that Jesus gave the apostles, the first priests, the power to both forgive and to hold sins fast (and the power required for all the sacraments). This underscores Jesus's intent for us to humble ourselves and to show we truly are contrite, or sorry, by verbally expressing our sins to a priest. The priest can withhold absolution if he does not feel the person is truly sorry. Some may ask, "then why does the Church allow general confessions and general absolution?"

General confessions and absolutions are only supposed to be granted under extreme conditions (i.e. on the battlefield, a sinking ship, during a natural disaster for the affected people, etc.) and the absolution is only valid, if all other normal confession terms are met. These absolutions are granted with the understanding that when and if you can, you will go and make a personal confession as soon as you can (particularly crucial for absolution of mortal sin). Personal confessions are an important means of receiving absolution and Jesus's sanctifying grace.

On a personal level, I can truly relate to why Jesus instituted the Sacrament of Reconciliation as an alternative to simply talking directly to Jesus and asking for his forgiveness. I remember when my wife and I were visiting my daughter in college and we attended a Christmas Glee Club concert she had raved about. It was awesome! The concert did not start until late on Saturday night, so we decided to go to Saturday night mass. Given that it was the beginning of Advent and that we had extra time, we decided to go to confession. Even though it was only a few months since my last confession, I had plenty to share with the priest. I felt so good after confessing and receiving absolution I thought about this very question.

I have a habit of asking forgiveness of any sins I have before I receive communion at mass. Here I am talking directly to God. However, the act of humbling yourself, either behind a screen or face-to face with the priest, to God's middleman, another human being, was humbling but in the end so much more meaningful and gratifying. This priest was very good and very encouraging (he prompted me for even more potential sins). The act of verbalizing my sins to another person made my confession much more real and my repentance much more meaningful. Furthermore, I find myself much more capable of resisting my natural desire to repeat certain transgressions as a direct result of this very overt act of having to confess to a priest. So, I think Jesus, a.k.a. God, really knew what he was doing when he instituted this sacrament. And of course, we are blessed with an all loving and all merciful God!

43. How does the Catholic Church choose who becomes saints? A related question was, "How does a person become a saint?"

There are many good Catholic sources (including Fr. Robert Spitzer's *Credible Catholic* modules) that can answer the more literal interpretation of the question as to how persons are officially recognized or canonized as saints in the Catholic Church. The process is a rigorous one for these persons become both intercessors for us and serve as role models for us. I won't dwell on this more literal aspect, rather I will focus on what I believe these questions are really speaking to, which is the more general point of how some human beings can rise so clearly above the masses despite being born like all other human beings.

However, before answering your literal question, allow me to point out a key aspect of sainthood. All those who die and go to heaven become saints. So, we are all aspiring saints or "saints in training" here on earth.

Fr. John A. Hardon explains in *The Catholic Catechism* that, "In the canonization process, the Church wants to make sure that those who are raised to the honors of the altar (canonized as saints) had either suffered martyrdom or, during life, had practiced such heroic virtue that they are worthy of emulation by the faithful. Among other qualities of heroic virtue are such features as cheerful endurance of great suffering, unflinching confidence in God in spite all human expectations, and a selfless love of others in the face of trial and persecution". So clearly only a very elite group ever become officially recognized by the Church as saints and the process is long, thorough and rigorous. It is a real exacting vetting or due diligence process.

But first, how do ordinary men and women develop the qualities that enable them to become saints? Why them and not us? Noting the qualifications above, be careful what you wish for, are you up to the task? In this question lies the answer to "why them?". Fr. Hardon cites the "making" of a saint this way:

> "It is not a passing remark that when the Council of Trent described justification as a "renovation of the interior man through the **voluntary** reception of grace," since our free wills have much to do with setting limits to divine generosity. St. Francis de Sales observed that it is the measure to which we divest ourselves of self-love, so that our heart does not refuse consent to the divine mercy God "ever pours forth and ceaselessly spreads his sacred inspirations, which ever increases and makes us increase more in more in heavenly love." He then asks how it happens that we are not so advanced in the love of God as some of the saints: "It is because God has not given us the grace. But why has he not given us this grace? Because we did correspond with his inspirations as we should have. And why did we not correspond? Because being free we have herein abused our liberty." Living in grace, therefore, is a vital process from the divine side and ours: God is free to confer this life and in the degree that pleases his unfathomable will, and we are free to receive what he offers and as much as we choose according to our own generosity."

Fr. Hardon is telling us that we decided on our own not to accept the same graces that were made available to the saints before us. This also explains why we sin and sin to varying levels of seriousness or degree. We all have free wills and we all have God's grace made available to us. Some are stronger than others to resist temptation, to succumb to peer pressures, to go with the flow instead of standing firm and accepting the grace made available, as well as accepting the trials and tribulations that may accompany this gift.

Fr. Hardon describes the Church's view of saints as, "In the life of those who share our human nature yet become more completely changed into the likeness of Christ (saints), God makes his presence, his countenance, vividly manifest to men. In their person he addresses us, he offers us the standard of his kingdom, and we who are surrounded by so great a cloud of witnesses, such a proof of the Gospel's truth, we are powerfully attracted to it."

This is another reason the Church is careful about which human beings they canonize as saints. They are important role models for us and must be real, not put on or made up in any way.

Regarding the question of how miracles are performed by or associated with saints. We must remember these saints are all human beings and any powers they have or acts they are able to perform are not done by them but thru them by God himself. St. Paul could not of his own ability heal the sick, free himself from chains and imprisonment or convert so many to Christ. He, and all other saints like him, did these as God's instrument, in God's name.

44. Why don't other Christian faiths believe in saints?

Other Christian faiths do not recognize human beings as saints like Catholics do and do not pray to them to intercede for them, for non-Catholic Christians feel that to do so detracts from the worship of God. They feel we as Catholics, worship these saints and that as sinners they should not hold the same place of honor and worship as our Lord and savior Jesus Christ. I will not speak to specific non-Christian faiths as the reasons could vary dramatically by faith denomination.

First, I have trouble with the word "worship". We do not worship them like gods or golden idols and we certainly do not treat them as equals to Jesus Christ. We pray to them to intercede on our behalf with Jesus. We also acknowledge their unique qualities that led to them being canonized as saints. We are not putting them ahead of, or equal to God. We believe they are in heaven and can act as our advocates, our intercessors with God. Also, many find it easier to pray to a saint who was human like us and may have led a life that we can personally relate to and can therefore more readily pray to them to intercede on our behalf. This is especially true of Mary.

Catholics do not worship Mary (even though she is believed to have been born without sin and to never have committed a sin) or the saints, we are praying in communion with them. We are asking them to intercede for us. We are not asking or expecting them to directly answer our prayers. We are asking them, to ask God, to answer our prayers. We know by the example of the miracle of the Wedding feast of Cana that Jesus will not say no to his mother. Mary and the saints are all like us, they are human and are part of the "mystical body of Christ". As we are all part of the same body, we all should work in harmony and support each other, for it is always better for the whole body, to work for the well-being of one of the parts. What I have found interesting is that in conversations with other Christians, they have asked for my prayers and have offered their prayers for me or for others who were in particular need, dealing with serious life challenges. They were offering their intercessory prayer, just as we Catholics do when we appeal to Mary or the saints. We are not worshipping Mary or the saints, we are honoring them and seeking their help.

45. Is a bishop a bishop from the start or do they work up to it?

Generally speaking, bishops are priests who are in essence, ordained to a higher order in the hierarchy of the Church. Bishops can become archbishops (this usually correlates with responsibility for a larger diocese in terms of Catholics in the flock, or the population in the geographic area covered by each diocese) and could ultimately become the Pope. Bishops must exhibit a certain set of skills or abilities, just like an employee moving up the corporate ladder in a business environment. Today, bishops must be good priests as well as good administrators and communicators and usually have strong interpersonal skills. However, bishops' skill sets on each of these and other important areas can and do vary. Bishops, like popes, pastors and all priests seek to surround themselves with other clergy and laity to help them, particularly in areas where they may not be as proficient as they want to be or feel they need to be. They are no different than anyone of us in the sense that we are all born with varying talents, gifts (charisms) and abilities. We are all part of the "Mystical Body of Christ" and as such, have our own unique roles to play. That is, if we are an "ear" in this body we need to rely on someone else who is an "eye" for sight.

46. Can you visit people here on earth if you have died and gone to heaven?

The short answer is no! We learned from the parable of the rich man who daily sat at his window and ate and drank abundantly but did not share his bounty, his gifts from God with a beggar who tried daily in vain to obtain just the leftovers or remnants from the rich man's lavish feasts. When the rich man died and went to hell (the corollary of your question), the rich man begged God from his pain and suffering state in hell to allow him to leave hell, even if for just a brief time to warn his brothers to live differently than he did. God refused him and basically said, if your brothers would not listen to my son, Jesus Christ, they surely won't listen to you! On another level, when we die, it is our souls that initially go to heaven or hell based on our own particular judgment while our bodies whither, decay and turn to dust. We are not re-united with our resurrected bodies until the Final Judgment at the end of time.

47. How does God choose when and how people die? A related question was, "Why does God make the decision to let some people die young?

People often question how an all-powerful (omnipotent) and all knowing (omniscient) supreme being, like our God, can let bad things happen, to good people? How can he let a newborn child die or an unborn child die in the womb? How can he let evil reign and corrupt us, tempt us to make bad choices and let people get hurt or killed by natural disasters or other human caused events?

I watched my good friend, Jim Harrell, who battled a very debilitating disease called ALS, also known as Lou Gehrig's disease, slowly, over a seven-year period die from this disease. Like dying on a cross, you eventually die from your lung muscles weakening so much that you cannot breathe, unless in your weakened state, death is brought on by some other cause. Jim was near my age, had four great children, and a beautiful loving wife. He died on January 8th, 2010 and he did not live long enough to see his children marry or see his grandchildren. Gradually over this period his muscles began to fail, to atrophy, until he could not walk, so he was then confined to a wheelchair. His muscles continued to deteriorate to the point he was confined to a bed. Ultimately, he became almost fully paralyzed. His mind remained as sharp as a tack throughout this process but eventually he could barely move his mouth muscles to verbally communicate before he finally died.

However, despite being afflicted with this cruel disease over this long and difficult seven-year period, Jim carried his cross positively and never blamed, complained, or "got mad" at God. In fact, Jim went out of his way to speak all over the area to encourage people to joyfully accept whatever crosses they were carrying in their own lives. He was a very encouraging, positive influence on all who met or knew him.

Similarly, a good friend of mine and his wife, John and Linda, had their five-year-old son contract a rare brain disease. He was hospitalized, hundreds of tests were run, no specific disease was identified, and no cure was found. Then, miraculously he seemed nearly one hundred percent cured. He went home and even went back to school for a while, but only a short time later the symptoms reappeared and within weeks of his sixth birthday he died. How does an all-powerful God let these things happen? This roller coaster ride of sickness and then apparent healing to such a young child was extremely difficult for John and Linda to bear. They struggled to understand why an all loving, all powerful and all merciful God would let this happen to their little boy.

Randy Alcorn, an author I have referenced multiple times already, wrote an excellent book entitled *If God is Good*. I cannot replicate adequately in a few sentences the profound insights and wisdom into God's plan that Randy details in this great four hundred fifty-page book. I can tell you my friend Jim asked me to read this book to him from start to finish while he lay nearly paralyzed in his bed. Jim found great comfort in Randy's words and confirmed all the principles and points Randy made in this book as it related to his own experience. Jim died the afternoon after he heard the last few paragraphs from this book. Randy does a great job of explaining how God permits evil to happen and uses it for his own greater purpose. He explains why it is important that God lets his highest creation, man, whom he gave the unique gifts of a free will and intellects, to make good or bad, right or wrong decisions in their lives without his interference.

We would not be the high life forms we are if God treated us as robots or totally controlled our hearts and minds. We would be no better than animals or plants without these special gifts and without the supreme or god-like nature we each were uniquely blessed with…our souls. There are consequences or ramifications for all mans' decisions, both good and bad. Some of the consequences of the bad decisions are that bad things happen. This includes good angels like Lucifer turning away from God and in turn tempting us to turn away as well.

Jesus made the ultimate sacrifice by dying on the cross for us, so God the Father let the ultimate bad thing happen to his own Son. He did so because it was all part of his greater plan, a plan we cannot begin to appreciate or comprehend with our limited mortal intellects. However, God promised that if we had faith, if we accepted his calling and his will for us, good or bad, and endeavored to live a good life consistent with his wishes, that we would have eternal happiness, a happiness that goes beyond our wildest imagination. We simply need to accept the challenges he presents us with, or that others inflict upon us, and the grace he gives us to live though those challenges.

I would also encourage you to review Fr. James Spitzer's seventh module in his *Credible Catholic* series. This module does a great job of covering why an all- powerful, all loving God, allows pain and suffering in our human world.

48. Can a person lose their soul?

Your soul is created by God the Father through the Holy Spirit, at the moment you were conceived. Your soul is the one aspect of our human natures that is "God-like" or that most resembles his image and likeness. Our souls are not physical in nature, so they can never die, be taken, lost or stolen…at least not in the literal sense of the word.

God made us to know him, to love him, to serve him and to be eternally happy with him in heaven. When we sin, or turn away from God, we lose sanctifying grace and our souls become spiritually weak. If we commit mortal or grave sins, we could effectively end our "Communion with God" separating ourselves from him. However, we can reverse this condition and restore our communion with him through the Sacrament of Reconciliation (provided we are truly sorry for any sins at the point of receiving this sacrament and by the forgiving, merciful nature of our Savior Jesus Christ).

This can also be achieved through the Sacrament of Anointing of the Sick. So, our souls can become spiritually bankrupt or dead and then are in a sense "lost". However, they can be found again and brought back to life through these sacraments coupled with a truly contrite heart and a commitment not to continue in our sinful ways and to due penance or restitution for our sinful ways.

49. Why do you have to be a certain age to receive the Sacrament of Holy Communion (the Sacrament of Holy Eucharist)?

Thankfully the Church recognizes that at an early age we have sufficient reasoning power to know right from wrong and that we should choose to do the right thing...even if we know we are not strong enough to consistently choose to do the right thing. We first receive the Sacrament of Reconciliation as early as age seven (second grade) and then months later, after much preparation, we are allowed to receive the Sacrament of Holy Eucharist. So, while our understanding of, and appreciation for, these two sacraments may still be rather rudimentary at age seven, Jesus Christ, through the inspiration and actions of our Catholic Church, felt that at this age we "can be ready enough".

The belief is that it is better to begin to reap the sanctifying graces as early on as reasonably possible that accrue to us from these sacraments, rather than wait until later when we might more deeply appreciate the sacraments before reaping these benefits. I admit my own appreciation and understanding of the "power" and "gift" of the Holy Eucharist has grown over time and that on any given day at mass my "awareness" of this gift varies in degree, but I am most thankful for the daily opportunity to "receive".

50. What do the letters on the head of the cross mean?

Pontius Pilate, upon succumbing to the pressures and demands of the Jewish leaders, priests and people to crucify Jesus for blaspheming, for saying that he was God, the messiah, the promised king that was to come, insisted that the inscription "I.N.R.I" be posted over Jesus' head for all by-standers and passers-by to see. It was shorthand or an acronym that translated from Latin literally read: "Jesus the Nazarian, the King of the Jews", as it was the custom to place a sign stating the crucified's offense on the cross in Latin, Greek, and Hebrew. The leading Jewish priests said to Pilate, "Change it from, *The King of the Jews* to, *He said, I am King of the Jews.*" Pilate replied, "What I have written, I have written."

This was Pilate's attempt to put the Jewish leaders in their place and to acknowledge, in a backhanded way, that maybe this really was the King of the Jews. The Jewish leaders did not like this at all but were powerless to do anything about it! So, it was ironic that a Roman authority recognized Jesus for who he was and yet was not strong enough to protect Jesus for simply stating the truth. At the same time Jesus, a Jew and a Nazarene, was being handed over to the Romans for death by his fellow Jews and towns people.

51. Do Catholics want to someday reunite with protestants?

I personally believe Catholics do want to reunite with people of all faith denominations and vice versa. The question is will it be here on this mortal and humanly limited earth or will it be in heaven…possibly on a new, glorified earth? On this mortal earth we strive for one universal Church, but this may not be achievable in any of our mortal lifetimes given our human failings and foibles. However, the Catholic Church certainly looks forward to bridging the gap now without sacrificing core dogmatic positions and to the Final Judgment when the only dividing line will be those who have achieved eternal salvation and a life with Christ versus those that have rejected God and are dammed to a life devoid of Christ.

The Church today focuses more on the similarities rather than on the differences we have with other faith denominations. I used to attend a Thursday morning men's meeting at a local Christian Church at the invitation of my neighbor. I went consistently for a long period of time as I was able to relate to other men of faith, hear interesting speakers and to discuss common beliefs. I eventually stopped attending after I became known as the "Lone Catholic" and when too much of our dialog focused on the differences between Catholics and Christians in a group setting that clearly would not result in either side changing their core beliefs. These men all believed Jesus was the Son-of-God, so I decided to shift my time and focus on reaching out to people who did not know or accept Jesus as our Savior. I have had opportunities to join with other Christians in this effort and will continue to look for others!

52. How does the New Testament and the Old Testament correlate to each other?

First the Old Testament is that portion of the Bible (Sacred Scripture or The Word) that covers the period of the creation of our universe up to the birth of Jesus Christ. The New Testament is all Sacred Scripture beginning with, and after, the birth of Jesus Christ. The Catholic Church recognizes forty-six Old Testament books and twenty-seven books in the New Testament for a total of seventy-three books. The Catholic Church recognizes seven more books than are recognized in the Jewish Bible. These include Tobit, Judith, First and Second Maccabees, Wisdom, Sirach and Baruch as the Jews accepted only those books known at the time to have been written in Hebrew. More recently, documents were found that suggest many of these "additional" books were in fact written in Hebrew.

However, there are real correlations between the Old and New Testaments. Many of the New Testament authors directly and indirectly relate Jesus's teachings and deeds to Old Testament writings and prophecies. Jesus became man for many reasons other than to overcome sin and death. He came to fulfill Old Testament prophecies and he came to change old laws or old ways. He also came to enhance his relationship with his people. He wanted to build on the Ten Commandments and show by example how we are to live our lives', how we are to treat others. He came not only to remind us to follow his laws but to show us how we should live our lives. He led by example and he gave us the Beatitudes which are eight "directives" on things we "should do" while the Ten Commandments are essentially "things we should NOT do". So, it is more about how we should treat others, for as we treat others, so we treat Christ, for Christ is in each one of us. This is also why he gave us the Great Commandment when asked which of the Ten Commandments was the most important. Jesus gave us one new law, albeit with two main parts. "You shall love the Lord your God, with all your heart, with all your being, with all your strength, and with all your mind, AND love your neighbor as yourself" (Lk 10:27). If we model our lives to the fullest around this Great Commandment, we will by default follow all his other laws and commandments.

On another level, there are indeed many correlations between Old Testament persons, places, things and events to counterpart persons, places, things and events in the New Testament. We call these Old Testament persons or things "prefiguring's" or "parallels". The New Testament counterpart is always superior to its Old Testament prefiguring, like Mary was to Eve.

The Old Testament is filled with prophecies that are subsequently fulfilled in the New Testament. Jesus fulfilled over three hundred different Old Testament prophecies in his thirty-three short years on earth. I always wish I could have been one of the disciples that met Jesus on the road from Jerusalem to Emmaus on the day Jesus rose from the dead (Read Chapter 24 of Luke's Gospel). Jesus approached the two disciples but did not reveal who he was to them and pretended to know nothing about "Jesus" and his recent crucifixion. Jesus asked them, "What is this conversation that you are holding with each other as you walk" (Lk 24:17)? Then as they walked and talked Jesus revealed to them all the prophecies of the Old Testament and how they were fulfilled through his life, words, actions, crucifixion and death. He then revealed himself to them at table as he consecrated the bread and wine. The two disciples were so excited they immediately returned to Jerusalem in the darkness of night. How cool must that experience have been??

53. Are we as Catholics the only church that is opposed to abortion and believe that a fetus contains a soul given by God at conception?

This is a two-part question. The answer to the first part is that there are many churches who are opposed to abortion. These include Christian and non-Christian religions. A personal regret of mine is that these churches do not play a more active role and better leverage their political clout in their resistance to abortion and working against the election of pro-abortion politicians.

Science has learned so much more about the development of a fetus since the Supreme Court's Roe vs. Wade decision on abortion and how soon after conception the fetus has real discernable human features. Yet despite this scientific knowledge, and despite most of us and most religions' belief that human life begins at conception, abortion remains legally viable in the United States and in many other countries worldwide. This is a real travesty! I hope that in my lifetime we will see a reversal of this decision just as years ago the U.S. passed legislation ending the travesty of slavery.

As to the second part, the dogma of being conceived both with body and a soul is more unique to Christian faith denominations but is not limited to them. I am not enough of an expert to provide a definitive list.

54. I have not had the consecrated wine, God's blood ever since my First Communion, is it bad that I have not received the blood for so long (I still take the consecrated bread, God's body)?

No, it is not wrong at all and you are not any less receiving Christ in this sacrament by only receiving communion under one form versus both forms or species, as it is also referenced. In fact, for a long time, receiving Christ under both forms was limited to special events like First Communions, Easter, Christmas, etc. Now it is more common to have the option of receiving the Holy Eucharist under both forms of body and blood. However, even in these parishes, with more health concerns during the flu season, many that offer the consecrated wine (the blood of Christ) from a common cup, cease offering this option.

Similarly, it matters not if you have a whole host or a partial host. Any portion size or any species of consecrated material is sufficient for fully receiving Christ and all the possible graces that accrue from properly participating in this sacrament. This is important for the elderly or anyone that may have difficulties swallowing when it is better for them to consume only a small portion of a host. Of course, receiving only His precious blood might be a better alternative if receiving under both species is an option. Many Catholic Churches do not offer both species during flu season or on weekdays or only on special days in larger parishes.

55. The following questions were very similar and are answered as one below.

Why did God tell Adam and Eve not to eat from that one tree (even though he already knew they were going to do it?)? If God has such incredible powers, why didn't he prevent Adam and Eve from sinning?

How could God be all powerful but not change the problems we have today?

Genesis, the first book of the Bible, reminds us that God created human beings above all his other creations and gave us "dominion over" these lesser creations but this was not just in name or position. He gave us three attributes that differentiate us from all other life forms (plants and animals). He gave us free wills, intellects and souls. God did this with his full supremely omniscient (all knowing) and omnipotent (all powerful) natures. He knew full well that these gifts would be used both positively and negatively and that there would be consequences to our having these unique gifts. He did so anyway to create a special life form that more closely approximated his own divine nature and out of an unbelievable love he has for each one of us. We were made in his "image and likeness". It is our soul that most closely resembles "His Image". God always was and always will be. So, like him, our souls will never die. However, he also gave us intellects and free wills, so we could discern things for ourselves and freely make choices. He knew we would not always make good choices, but he did not want us to be like animals or robots. He wanted to give us the ability and power to know and to choose how we would live our lives, to decide to do right things or wrong things, and to know the difference.

Just because he knows ahead of time what decisions we will make; these are no less our decisions. Our lives are pre-known by God but not predetermined by God. If I could travel in time and see who would win this year's Super Bowl and then return to the present time, my knowledge of who would win would in no way affect all the individual decisions the coaches and players ultimately make on what plays to run and how to run them. Our lives are not predetermined, predestined or out of our control just because God knows in advance what decisions we will make.

God knew we would not always use this gift wisely. Just like he created Lucifer, and the other angels who rebelled against God and were ultimately forced out of heaven by St. Michael, God does not control how we use the gifts he gives us. He knew we would make bad decisions and that there would have to be consequences for these bad decisions. Randy Alcorn reminds us in his book, *If God is Good*, that God did not create evil, nor does he cause evil, but he does permit evil to exist and he uses evil things and evil people for his ultimate purpose. Some of the consequences of evil or bad decisions are pain, suffering and death. However, Jesus, the Son of God, paid the ultimate sacrifice for all our bad or evil ways by humbling himself, becoming man and then letting us torture and crucify him so he could rise and conquer sin and death. This was all part of his plan of "redemptive salvation".

Like Job from the Old Testament, or others you may know, like my good friend Jim Harrell who died of ALS, also known as Lou Gehrig's disease, which is a very difficult, debilitating disease, that despite much focus by researchers and doctors for a cure, as of this writing, always results in death. God calls many of us to carry an extra burden by asking us to accept challenges in our lives', so we too can participate in his overall plan of redemptive salvation. Like other choices we are enabled to make, we can either accept these challenges willingly and gracefully and use them as gifts to help others and give honor and glory to God (as my friend Jim Harrell did), or we can turn bitter and cry, "why me God"?

Back in the Old Testament times, people did not understand this. They felt that anyone who was afflicted with a disease or a handicap, a physical impairment of some kind, that this was given to them as a direct consequence for their own personal sin or that of their parents. They did not understand God's real plan. Pain and suffering are consequences for the general sinful nature of man. They are also a consequence of our mortal natures or of the uninhibited nature of nature itself. And, while God asks some to carry heavier burdens of pain and suffering, he does so with a plan and a purpose. God provides extra blessings of faith, grace and inner strength to help the suffering deal with the burden they have been asked to carry. Not all respond well and accept the burden and the graces for what they really are. These challenges present growth opportunities for ourselves and opportunities to help others achieve salvation by the example we can set, by willingly accepting these challenges and using them for God's greater honor and glory.

The forbidden fruit of the tree even in the Garden of Eden, real or parabolic, was symbolic of our ability to choose right from wrong to use God's gift of a free will. Don't you think if Adam and Eve had not eaten of the fruit that there would have soon been some other transgression that one of us would have committed? So, like the number forty in the Bible as a sign of the author not being totally sure of the actual amount of time that had passed, it does not matter what the actual first sin was or who committed it, but rather that it underscores our weak human natures and our reliance on an all merciful, forgiving and loving God for salvation? And, while a fully omnipotent, all powerful God could prevent any of us, at any given point in time, from sinning or having some natural disaster hurt or kill us, he chooses to let us exercise our free will as part of a much bigger plan than we cannot fully comprehend with our limited human intellects. However, after the Final Judgement Day, when we are enjoying eternal life in heaven, God's full plan will become known to us.

56. Does the Catholic Church believe in extraterrestrial life?

I could not find any definitive church position on this question. However, one thought is that if there really are life forms equivalent to that of humans, that is, with free wills, intellects and souls, they will have the same potential to get heaven as we do.

They too have been redeemed by nature of the Son of God becoming man and dying to redeem us from the pain and eternal damnation of our sinful ways. If they had free wills, undoubtedly someone went south and made a bad decision. The other option is God made a similar but different life form and maybe they are different enough that a whole different plan of salvation is required but I am too human and too limited to conceive of just how that all could be.

57. What would have happened if Mary had said no to Jesus? And another similar question: What would have happened if Lucifer hadn't turned on God?

These are interesting hypothetical questions, but I would argue that fundamentally nothing would have been different. For with Mary, God would have known through his supreme, omniscient nature, whether or not Mary was "up to the challenge" and know if she would have positively responded to his call or his will for her or not. And, with Lucifer, if the implication is that we would not have had a devil if Lucifer had remained true to God and then God would not have had to overcome sin, evil and death, I believe there probably would have been another like him? One of his current underlings would have risen to the occasion.

So, an all-powerful God would have been able to create another "gunae", another woman, that would have been strong enough to respond positively to his call had he known that Mary would decline his request. Or, he would have another way to become man, to become incarnate. If you believe God is powerful enough to create our universe out of nothing, isn't it plausible that God could have devised a "Plan B" (which would have really been a Plan A given his omniscient nature)?

In no way does this take away from the totally awesome strength and will power of Mary to say yes to the Angel Gabriel. Mary, as only a fourteen-year-old girl, said yes, knowing that she could have been stoned to death for having a child outside of marriage, for "she knew not man". We know this means she had already dedicated her life to God and planned to remain a virgin, but she still accepted God's call for her to be the Mother of Jesus and have it done to her according to God's will. This does not mean that Mary did not freely decide to say yes to God's call. It simply means God knew she would say yes. He would not have sent the Angel Gabriel to Mary had he not known how she would respond.

58. I am confused because I have heard that Jesus is God's son and that God is Jesus. I always understood Jesus is God's son.

So, you are correct on both points in your question. Jesus is indeed God's son and Jesus, as one of three "persons" in the Trinity is also fully divine, is God. Jesus is the Son of God the Father. So, while there is one God, there are three divine persons in one God. That is, God has three fully unique persons or natures, God the Father, God the Son (a.k.a. Jesus), and God the Holy Spirit. These three persons or natures in one are referred to as the Holy Trinity. So, when God wanted to overcome sin and death and "crush the head of the serpent" as promised in Genesis, he agreed to sacrifice his only Son, by allowing him to become man and ultimately be beaten and crucified as atonement for all the sins of mankind. So, the Son of God became the "Word Incarnate", the "Word made Flesh" and "dwelt among us" in human form known as Jesus. Jesus, the Son of God, was both fully man and fully divine or God.

These are not easy concepts to explain, let alone understand and require the gift of faith to accept as true. However, they do underscore the depth of God's love for us if you think about the love required to suppress all the powers of omniscience and omnipotence and to sacrifice an only divine son so all of God's creatures had the opportunity to one day be happy with him in heaven.

59. Do you always have to pray to get into heaven?

Taking your question literally and at the most general level the answer is a qualified no but be careful and read on. I must clarify my answer here is a personal one and not necessarily a documented position of the Catholic Church. However, I expect, while it would be expressed in a more profound way than I am able to do here, the Church would officially answer in a similar manner.

Let me first explain my initial macro level answer, that technically you need not pray at all to get to heaven. Many of our counterparts from other Christian faith denominations would tell you that you simply must accept Jesus Christ as your Lord and Savior to get to heaven. Some go even further and suggest that it matters not how you live your life; it only matters that you accept Jesus Christ as your Lord and Savior. So strictly following this doctrine, prayer would technically be totally unnecessary to get to heaven. Furthermore, there are many unborn babies (who we firmly believe to be fully human at conception), young babies and children as well as those that never knew Christ or had the opportunity to learn or know about prayer.

How could you possibly accept Jesus Christ as your Lord and Savior if you do not "know" him, are not in "relationship" with him. This comes from learning about him formally (school or in private study and informally through your parents, by reading the Bible, talking to Jesus, doing kind acts for others, and regularly participating in all the sacraments that are available to you…. to name only a few. Guess what, each one of these is a form of prayer! When we truly are in "relationship" we feel compelled to return the love shown to us. We return His love through all these various forms of prayer. Through this love we are infused with a sense of charity, we put the needs of others first and we are then able to more closely love others as Jesus showed us how to love.

So yes, you absolutely should pray to be in relationship with Jesus, to get to heaven and to maximize that experience once you get there. However, you get to pick the form and frequency of prayer forms you want to use. There are many forms of prayer, only some of which I have already mentioned. One last point, if I focus for a minute on the form of prayer that may have been behind your question, I cannot encourage this enough. We have so many competing messages (messages that lead us away from God) coming to us from smart phones, TV, movies, the internet, magazines, newspapers and society in general, we need to balance this with other "god-pointing" messages. We all need quiet time away from the harangue of these competing messages to stay focused, to build that relationship with Jesus. But don't forget to ask the Holy Spirit, Mary and the other saints, to intercede on your behalf when you are asking for help in your life.

Start now to make time in the morning before you get up and again before you go to bed at night, to talk to God in your own words or through rote prayer. I like to end each day while I am lying in bed and after I have said my formal prayers or had my talk with God, to reflect on the day that just ended. I try to think of things I did wrong or the times I did not behave or respond to situations as best I could have. How would Jesus have reacted in those same situations. I then try to think of things I thought went well, that I was pleased with. I thank the Holy Spirit for his grace and help achieving those pleasing outcomes and for the grace and strength to do even better the next day!

Lastly, don't forget to say prayers of thanks for all God has blessed you with. Often, we focus our prayer time on "requests" and forget to balance them with prayers of thanks, praise, or just prayers of dialog with God. Tell him what is on your mind just like you would a close friend. Each day tell God you are dedicating all your thoughts, words and actions for his greater honor and glory! Seriously making this conscience offering, turns everything you think, say, and do, that day into a grace giving prayer and reduces the chances you will decide to act poorly.

When you do talk directly to God, I believe there are five steps that should be followed for any good prayer session, no matter how short or long the session or on what form of prayer you use. I use these five steps, especially right after I receive Holy Communion and I return to my pew to guide and shape my dialog with God. The steps are as follows, (but know this can be done faster/shorter, or yes, even longer than my explanation takes):

1. Acknowledge or in some way, recognize and praise God's almighty, all powerful (omnipotent), supreme, and forgiving natures. Recognizing one or all these attributes of his, or some derivatives of these, are very appropriate. Tell him you know he hears and answers all our prayers and has the power to answer them in the time and manner that is best for us or the person(s) we are praying for.

2. Tell God you are sorry for any sins or transgressions you have committed and for help with any personality flaws you are looking to improve upon. Ask him for forgiveness for these sins and to look past these faults as he considers your prayerful requests. I think about how long it has been since my last confession and if more than a month I make a promise to God to get to the Sacrament of Confession/Reconciliation at the earliest possible time.

3. Thank God for all he has blessed you with and for all the previous prayers he has heard and answered. Too many times we ask God for things and forget to go back and thank him (don't be like the eight lepers Jesus healed, he healed nine but only one, the Samaritan leper returned to praise and thank Jesus). We also can't thank God enough for all the blessings he has bestowed upon us, without our even asking for them!

4. Now go ahead and ask Jesus first for those things you are seeking for others and then for your own personal intentions.

5. Finally, close by acknowledging that he may answer your prayers in a very different way than what you asked or expected. Also, let him know you understand his timeline may be a bit different than yours. Pray you will have the patience to wait for him to hear and answer your prayers and for understanding and acceptance when he answers your prayer in unexpected ways.

Matthew Kelly, the author of the *Decision Point* Confirmation preparation series, has a seven-step prayer process concluding with the prayer Jesus taught us, *The Our Father*. Can't go wrong ending your prayer session in this manner!

In addition, to praying for the day-to-day needs of those you know, for those you love, and for your own personal needs, you may want to consider praying for Jesus's help to be open to hearing and then to responding to his call or vocation for you in your life. Continually ask God what he wants you to be, what he wants you to do with your life. It may be to get married; it could be to remain single; or it could be a call to religious life. Too often we let our peers, or the media influence us instead of letting God be that influence. Just a thought!

Finally, you might think of occasionally praying for those who may not often be prayed for or may be forgotten all together. Some that come to mind include: the souls in Purgatory (that they soon may see God in heaven); for those who may be wavering in their faith or lack faith all together; for expectant parents and their unborn babies; for parents struggling to be blessed with the gift of a new healthy baby; for those seeking to adopt a child; for the elderly, particularly for those in nursing homes or extended care facilities; for those who are dying of terminal diseases and their families; for those without employment or those with jobs that are unfulfilling or do not pay adequately; for those who are infirmed, for those who are depressed (these numbers increase during the holidays), for politicians and world leaders, for the armed forces, for priests and nuns, for more religious vocations (we are at an all-time low in terms of young men and women responding to a call to religious life) and yes, why not throw in a few prayers for your full time teachers and while you're at it, how about one for your part time, volunteer Religious Education teachers as well.

60. Where did all the Catholic Church sacraments come from?

Each of the sacraments, of which there are seven, were instituted by Jesus Christ when he was here on earth. The sacraments are visible signs of Jesus's gifts to us and a means by which we can gain sanctifying grace. This grace helps strengthen us in our fight to resist the devil's attempt to steer us away from God and doing good acts, so he can get us to follow him by doing wrong or evil things. St. Paul cites his own weakness to resist the devil when he wrote, "For the good that I want, I do not do, but I practice the very evil that I do not want" (Ro 7:19). This is the power of the devil and the reason why we should regularly participate in all the sacraments available to us.

61. Was Jesus crucified on a Friday or is this just another detail that may not be historically accurate?

All four Gospel writers agree that Jesus died in the afternoon on the day before the Sabbath. The Sabbath for the Jewish people back then was always on a Saturday. Their days went from sunset to sunset so actually the Sabbath began on what would be our Friday evening right after sunset. The only area they all do not agree on is whether it was also the day before the beginning of Passover.

Passover occurs on the day of the first full moon of the spring equinox. Pentecost is always fifty days after Passover. Furthermore, all accounts agree that he was buried before sunset on Friday and that he rose from the dead two days later, or on the third day, a Sunday (Jewish first day of the week, like our Monday). Hope this is not too confusing!

62. How old was Joseph when he was with Mary and how close was Jesus to Joseph (his father)?

There is not much written about Joseph in the Bible and most of which is written about Joseph covers the time prior to Jesus starting his public life and most of this is from the period covering Jesus's birth through his teenage years. So, I should first clarify that Joseph was Mary's husband and Jesus's stepfather and the Holy Spirit was Jesus's actual father.

Joseph played a very important role in God's plan to have his Son Jesus become man and accomplish all that he did in his thirty-three short years on earth. Part of the reason we do not hear as much about Joseph lies in the fact that Jesus was only on earth for thirty-three years and only three of those years were spent preaching, teaching, performing miracles or in short living his "public life" which we now all know started with his first miracle at the wedding feast of Cana.

So, the New Testament focuses primarily on Jesus's life and teachings while he was here on earth. Remember I told you that John, one of the four gospel writers, made a point to remind us that not all could be written down about Jesus's life, teachings and surrounding events. However, all that was written was very important for our salvation and applicable, meaningful message-wise to all ages. Joseph's key role was/is as the head of the Holy Family and the fact that he agreed to marry Mary even though she was already pregnant, was extremely significant and sends a profound message to each one of us today. Joseph was believed to be a much older man, certainly much older than Mary who was believed to be about fourteen. Normally, Mary or any other woman, during Jesus's time, would have been stoned to death for being an unwed mother. Women who had children out of wedlock, before being married, were considered unclean.

In turn, it was considered inappropriate for a man to marry such an unclean person. However, Joseph responded to God's call through a dream where it was made clear to him that Mary was pregnant with the Son of Man as a result of the Holy Spirit overshadowing her. During this same dream, God asked Joseph to marry Mary (sounds funny) even though he knew Mary was committed to remaining a virgin. This would be a hard message for any of us to accept in today's day and age, let alone back in Jesus's time. Joseph was open to God's will and his specific call and responded. He became an excellent role model for all men of all ages and all generations regarding how to treat woman with respect and dignity and how to be a strong husband and father.

He also showed us the human side of Jesus as a son, to be strong, to have courage, to be open to God's plan for us and to respond to that call, no matter how hard or how different it is from what we think we want to be or do with our lives. One reason we have so few young men and woman responding to a call to the religious life as priests or nuns is not that there are any less calls by God to this life, but rather, it is that much harder for young men and woman to hear his call, let alone to respond in a positive manner! There are too many other competing or alternative messages from TV, movies, print media and our peers that serve to block our receptivity to God's call. This is one reason why we pray, so that we may hear and be open to God's call, to his will for us.

The explanation the Church gives for so little material on Joseph, for we do not hear about Joseph much after the "Finding of Jesus in the Temple" story when Jesus was twelve, is that this was not central to God' scriptural message. He inspired the scriptural authors to write what they wrote. Once the mystery of the virgin birth, the establishment of the Holy Family, etc was completed, the focus rightly shifts to Jesus's time on earth and all the follow-on messages, largely through apostolic letters, on the messages Jesus was communicating to those alive at that time but as well, for all generations to follow.

This also ties to the questions of whether Mary remained a virgin throughout her life, whether Mary and Joseph had other sons/daughters, and thus whether Jesus had brothers and sisters (the Bible references in multiple places "Jesus's brothers, sisters, family)". I have an excellent article that talks to this whole topic which I will not go into here but basically the Church has adopted St. Jerome's argument, the use and translation of the Greek word for "brothers" to be interpreted as meaning cousin(s), and that Mary was a perpetual virgin.

63. How can we get to heaven? I understand Jesus saves all and will save our non-Christian friends but, he also says that we must give up all our worldly possessions and give them to the poor to get to heaven. Correct?

Wow, very good, solid questions. Books have been written around these topics. I will try to give you my best balance of brevity and clarity but admit I am lacking in both areas.

So, as Catholics we believe we get to heaven by being baptized and confirmed (which is equivalent to other Christian denominations "accepting Jesus Christ as our Lord and Savior") through the Sacraments of Initiation and Acceptance. Then we must live our lives according to that faith. That is, we follow the Ten Commandments and the Beatitudes. In short, if we could consistently live our lives according to The Great Commandment, we would have a "confident assurance" that we would get to heaven. Jesus gave us this new commandment which has two key parts: First to Love God with our whole heart, mind and soul, and second, to love our neighbor as ourselves.

Many of our counterparts from other Christian faith denominations would tell you that you must accept Jesus Christ as your Lord and Savior to get to heaven. Some go even further and suggest that it matters not how you live your life; it only matters that you accept Jesus Christ as your Lord and Savior. How could you possibly accept Jesus Christ as your Lord and Savior if you do not know him and do not have a relationship with him. This comes from learning about him formally (in class or through a formal formation process) and informally through your parents, by reading the Bible, talking to Jesus (this is called prayer), doing kind acts for others, and regularly participating in all the sacraments available to you.... to name only a few.

The last area I have not covered is what is expected regarding our wealth or possessions. So, we are not expected to literally give away all our wealth. We are expected to give our time, talents and possessions to help those in need spiritually and corporally (physically). Jesus said it is harder for a rich man to get to heaven then for a camel to pass through the eye of the needle (reference to a low or narrow gate). He also said that the poor women who gave only the equivalent of pennies to the poor gave far more than those who had given exponentially more for she gave from her need while others gave from their excess. So, we are expected to follow the Beatitudes and help the poor but not to the extent that we cannot fulfill our other vocational responsibilities. Jesus knows that if we choose the vocation of parenthood and willing accept children into our marriage, that we must do so in a responsible manner. It costs time, talent and money to raise a family. We need to continually challenge ourselves to return or redirect the blessings God has bestowed on us to help others less fortunate for his greater honor and glory.

If you really want to challenge yourself in this area read the following books: *Happy are You Poor*, by Thomas Dubay and, *Not a Fan*, by Kyle Idleman. What Jesus is telling us is that we should put him first in our lives, regardless of our vocation in life. We should never have any kind of possession, activity or desire in life that is more important than our relationship with him.

64. Why are there less miracles today then back when Jesus was on earth?

So, what makes you think he does not continue to perform miracles every day and that they are not even more numerous than what we read about in the Bible? While he may not be physically present here in a human form, he is here with us as God in his divine nature and works both directly and indirectly through each of us.

Ask nurses and doctors who work in hospitals if they do not often see sick people recover that medically had been given no chance for recovery. Look at all the very good deeds and kind acts performed every day. Read about the life of Mother Theresa. Several new saints were more recently canonized including Blessed Mother Theodore Guerin from Terre Haute, IN. Pope John Paul II was canonized a saint as well. In fact, there is a great book on John Paul entitled, *Saint John Paul the Great,* by Jason Evert. Jesus works through us, through you and me as saints in training just as he did with his apostles!

Jesus's miracles are all around us and performed everyday by him through answered prayers, gifts bestowed on us and by him acting through others like the saints and other very good Christians. Unfortunately, bad news sells better on TV and rarely do our news programs focus on all the very good and positive things that happen daily in our world. Also, remember what Jesus said to Thomas after he appeared to the disciples a second time. Thomas was not there the first time Jesus appeared to his disciples after he arose from the dead and Thomas could not believe Jesus rose from the dead until he actually saw and touched Jesus (he wanted to see the miracle not just hear about it). Jesus said to Thomas, on the occasion of his second visit, "Happy are those, who do not see, yet believe". He was not just talking to Thomas, he was also talking directly to you, to me, and to all of those who have yet to come.

We must remember that God is always with us. His human nature may not be physically here on earth, but his divine nature certainly is. He is all around you, with you, and there for you. All we must do is "knock" and the door will be opened. Sometimes he may be "slower getting to the door" than we would like, and he may choose to answer your knock differently than you would like. He left us seven sacraments, he taught us how to pray, and he promised us he would always be with us. We need to pray, to develop a close working relationship with him by always talking to him and by learning more about our faith. We receive grace (help) through prayer, through active participation in mass and through the other sacraments that are open to us. Our challenge is to understand that God's will or plan for us, or for others whom we love, and for whom we may be praying, may be different than our wills, wants and expectations. Also, his timetable may be very different than ours. Some believe God is not listening or responding because he is not giving us what WE want, when WE want it. Au' contrair (thought I would throw some French in since all we have used is Aramaic and Greek in class, but I do not know French, so this may be off a bit??), he is listening and does respond. We may be the ones that are not hearing or responding.

Friendships take work, sacrifice, dialog and love. It is no different in our relationship with God. He made the ultimate sacrifice and shows us his love by being such a forgiving God. We need to uphold our end of the dialog and constantly seek out his help!

Finally, remember the parable of the rich man and Lazarus? Lazarus would sit outside the rich man's window starving, yet the rich man would never share any food with Lazarus, not even from his excess. Eventually the rich dude dies as does Lazarus. Lazarus goes to heaven and the rich man goes to hell. The rich man asks God to let Lazarus dip his finger in water and let the drips fall on his tongue as he is dying of thirst. Abraham explains that there is a barrier that prevents this from happening. So, then the rich dude asks Abraham to send Lazarus to warn his brothers that are still alive on earth. The rich man believes that if his brothers received a miraculous visit from the dead Lazarus that they would change their evil ways and not end up in hell like he did. Abraham's response was that if the rich man's brothers would not listen to the prophets or his own son who became man performed miracles, died and rose from the dead, they would not listen to Lazarus either!

I bring this up only to say that we have had miraculous things happen before, and while they continue to occur, even if not directly to us or ones we personally know, we must accept that miracles have and continue to happen. More importantly, we need to understand and respond to the significance of God's message that he is sending to us through the miracles performed in the past or in the present by him directly, or by those through whom God works.

I encourage to read the book entitled, *Where Angels Walk,* by Joan Wester Anderson. If you do not believe in angels or modern-day miracles you will after reading this book!

65. Why couldn't Jesus have used a word different than gunae when he addressed Mary? Why couldn't he have used the Hebrew or Aramaic word for mother?

So first let me clear up a few things. "Gunae" is the Greek word that means woman. I think what you are asking is why doesn't Jesus refer to Mary as "mother" or "mom" at any point during his time on earth? Why does he always use the Greek word for "woman"?

Remember that the first scholarly language that the Bible was written in was Greek. Jesus spoke Aramaic which is a derivative of Hebrew. When the Jewish people were in captivity their native Hebrew language evolved owing to their cultural interaction with their captors (Babylonians, Assyrians, et al). So, when Jesus spoke, he would have used the Aramaic word for woman.

So now that we cleared that up, I will answer the question I think you are asking. Jesus referred to his mother as woman not out of disrespect but as a way of communicating to us, generations later, re-enforcing that Mary was the woman (the gunae) promised to us and promised to the devil in the Old Testament after the devil tempted Adam and Eve to eat of the forbidden fruit. Remember God promised the devil that "a woman (a gunae) would come that would put enmity (hatred) between thy seed (the devil's) and her seed (referring to Mary and her son Jesus) and she will crush your head." Jesus is making it very clear that Mary is that gunae, that woman, who is fulfilling that Old Testament prophecy by continually referring to her by that name or title.

Remember, Jesus spent only three of his thirty-three years on earth revealing himself through his acts, his miracles and his teachings. Everything that Jesus said and did in that short time and everything written about Jesus in the New Testament (which is only a fragment of all that Jesus said and did) was very important. He wasted no words or actions and all his words and actions were messages to not only the people of his time but to all of those who would come later. He also knew (remember he was omniscient or all knowing, in addition to being omnipotent, all powerful) that there would be those throughout the ages that would question his messages and their meanings. So, he consistently used certain words, told specific parables and did all that he could on earth to help minimize the opportunity for misinterpretation.

However, remember that not EVERYTHING Jesus said or did on earth was written down in scriptures. This point is specifically made by John, one of the gospel writers, "There are also many things that Jesus did, but if these were to be described individually, I do not think the whole world would contain the books that would be written" (Jn 21:25). So, Jesus may very well, and more than certainly did, when he was younger and prior to commencing his public life, have referred to Mary as "mother" during his lifetime. However, during his three years of public life, he purposely used the word "gunae" to drive home the message I referenced above.

66. How did we get to all the different religions we have today?

So, I assume you are referring to the thousands of Christian denominations of faith that are active today (estimates range as high as twenty-six to thirty-three thousand Christian denominations alone). These large volumes of faith denominations are primarily an outgrowth of the Reformation led by Martin Luther when he broke away from the Catholic Church due to his problems with the current Pope Leo X and other personal issues he had relative to man's human nature to sin or to make bad choices. Martin Luther, along with others to follow in history, had a hard time accepting that popes, bishops and priests, like all other people are human beings and could be sinful and yet still be inspired by God and fulfill their priestly roles.

As we discussed, I could be a good teacher, a good policeman, a good salesman, a good doctor, but still have a weakness in one or more areas and be very sinful in these areas. This would not make me any less capable in my chosen profession. The same applies to the clergy in the Church. The Church has had and will continue to have popes, bishops, priests and nuns who have clearly had very observable human failings and weaknesses that are totally contrary to God's and our expectations of them. But this does not mean that they cannot still be good clergy persons.

Arguably, it is more surprising or difficult for us to understand these human weaknesses in our clergy because of the specific nature of the vocation they have responded to. We must remember that Jesus selected Peter as his first pope even though he knew that Peter would, in Jesus's greatest hour of need, deny Jesus three times. Jesus forgave Peter three times after he rose from the dead, to re-enforce the point that the leaders of the Church were human, could err, but could still be forgiven and still be effective Church leaders.

Okay, I will get back to answering the question, but I wanted to really hit home on this point since it was Martin Luther's loss of faith in the Pope and some of the practices at the time that helped drive him away from the Catholic Church. So, the real answer to the great number of "churches" or Christian faith denominations lie in the two key doctrines that started with Martin Luther and the Reformation. These are the doctrines of "sola fide" and "sola scriptura", by faith alone and by scripture alone. These two beliefs basically say that we do not need the Pope or the Magisterium (the teaching body) of the Church to interpret Sacred Scripture and apply it to our ever-changing world... despite the fact that Jesus clearly established this authority while he was here on earth.

Strict Reformationists would say we will look to Sacred Scripture and interpret it the way we believe it applies, we do not need the pope or the magisterium to interpret for us. They also would say it does not matter WHAT you specifically believe, only that you believe Jesus is the Son of God and that you have a personal relationship with Jesus. They also say, that it does not even matter HOW you live your life or HOW you ACT as long as, you believe in God. They say that to do so would suggest you can earn your way into heaven by doing kind acts. They say that our human failings are too great to ever be overcome by earning your way into heaven, so it does not matter how you act.

For all these reasons, different churches have been formed because each group or church selects the things "they" specifically believe in and how they want to act as a church, based on how they interpret and apply Sacred Scripture to the world or time they are currently living. We as Catholics would agree that we could not "earn" our way into heaven but that we do have a responsibility to "live" our faith and that it is through prayer and good acts that we grow and strengthen our faith and how we fulfill our responsibility as a faithful people to not just care for ourselves but for all members of the "mystical body" of Christ. We are all part of one body, of one Church and have an obligation to use the faith and the talents God gave us for his greater honor and glory. We do this through our thoughts, words and actions.

The Bible is more than a book, it is, per Bishop Barren's analogy, a library or a collection of books written by many different authors, over hundreds of years, with different cultural, historical, geographical and educational backgrounds. These books were written in many different styles (biographical, poetic, literal, parabolic, etc. and then written first in Greek and then Latin and ultimately translated or transliterated (close meaning words when directly translatable words were not possible). Without a solid knowledge and understanding of all these cultural, linguistic, geographical, historical nuances, it is very easy to misinterpret, misunderstand and misapply God's intended scriptural messages he intended the inspired biblical authors to convey.

Remember my example of our forefathers who left us the Constitution, the Bill of Rights, the three branches of government and the amendment process. They had enough foresight to know we needed a formal hierarchy and a living, breathing government structure that could grow and flex to our ever-changing world.

Don't you think Jesus had at least as much foresight as our forefathers?? Is it likely, after Jesus became man, died on the cross, and then rose from the dead, that he would then just leave us each to our own individual devices to try to figure out and apply his messages totally on our own, for ages and ages to come later???? No way!!! But that does not mean we do not have a responsibility to seek out these messages by reading scripture, meeting in groups to discuss their meaning and application, praying for wisdom, seeking out the Church's authoritative positions and seeking to understand why they are what they are, and then sharing these learnings with others in discipleship and witness? Yes of course we do!!!

67. What is the true meaning of the story of David and Goliath? Why do we fall into Satan's traps?

I could not find an authoritative answer so here is my personal view. The real short answers are: 1.) Don't mess with God or his chosen ones. And, 2.) Because we are mortal, human beings with weaknesses and imperfections, the powerful fallen angel (Lucifer a.k.a, Satan) actively and ceaselessly works to exploit those weaknesses and turn us away from God.

There is not much more I can add (but by now you know I cannot respond with a brief and succinct answer to just the specific question raised) other than to say that David was one of God's chosen ones, His first king of Israel, and that David, filled with courage, as inspired by God through the Holy Spirit, responded to God's call. So, the message is that God will give us the strength, the grace, and the power to fulfill his will. We need to be open to his calling (pray regularly for help to be listening for his call and then to separate our desires from his) and then finally, willingly, respond to his calling.

The devil's (St. Lucifer, the bad angel) sole objective is to recruit more bad angels, to turn us away from God by tempting us. He does this by making bad things, seem good to us. Remember this concept of sin is revealed to us through the story of how Satan tempted Eve to commit the first sin by telling her that by eating the fruit she would be "all knowing" or as smart as God. So, by appealing to Eve's vanity (this applies to all of us) or desire to be smarter, the devil successfully tempted her to sin. He is equally successful with us by appealing to our free wills (ability to make our own decisions) and to our human weaknesses. He tempts us to eat more than we should, to drink more than we should, to watch movies that we should not, and to disobey our parents (sometimes by using our very own friends or peers to help tempt us) by thinking it wouldn't be so bad to do something that your parents told you not to do (like stopping somewhere after school that you have been forbidden to go).

Remember, the devil is not really a person but an angel, he has no human form and never did. Satan, or St. Lucifer (sounds like an oxymoron doesn't it? look that word up or ask your parents what it means, how can the devil be a saint?). The first angels (also called saints because all saints are angels and all angels are saints, but that is a whole other topic) had a bit of power struggle in heaven. The bad angels, led by St. Lucifer, thought they were at least as good as, if not better than God. They found out otherwise and were banished from heaven, into what we know as hell (but be careful, hell is not a physical place).

All angels, even the bad ones have at least two things in common with us, they have spiritual natures called souls (which makes them and us, God-like, but not gods or God equivalents) and free wills. Lucifer decided, or exercised his free will, to turn from God and has remained so ever since. His spiritual nature has eternal qualities and thus never dies. So yes, he is symbolized as being bad for he, and his satanic disciples, are in fact bad and will always be banished to hell. But make no mistake, he has supernatural powers and will continually try to tempt us directly and indirectly to sin and turn away from God.

We are better equipped to resist his temptation by gaining sanctifying grace from participation in the sacraments, prayer and by doing our best to obey the Ten Commandments and live as Jesus asked us to do through the Beatitudes. I encourage you to read, *The Screwtape Letters*, by C.S Lewis for an interesting take on how the devil might work to lead us astray!

68. How could Jesus, and now priests, change bread and wine into His body and blood?

As the fifth Mystery of the Luminous Mysteries of the Rosary remind us, this was made possible (remember the Greek phrase the Angel Gabriel used in response to Mary's question, "How shall this be….that she would be the mother of Jesus for she knew not man?" was, "Pon Roma", or, "every word is not impossible….with God"…the Greeks loved to use double negatives for emphasis) because Jesus instituted the Sacrament of Holy Eucharist at the Last Supper. Jesus promised his disciples and to all those he preached, that to have eternal life you must eat his body and drink his blood. He reminded them that he fed their ancestors who wandered in the desert for forty years before reaching the promised land with bread from heaven, called manna. However, this bread fed their mortal bodies, but he offered them His body and blood that would feed their spiritual lives and allow them to "live forever". He was not talking about them literally biting off chunks of his skin or puncturing his body and drinking his blood. He was not promising that their weak, human, and mortal forms would not eventually die. He did promise that the transformed bread and wine he gave them would ensure their souls would be rejoined with a glorified body that would, along with their souls, live eternally with him in paradise.

Most did not understand then and many still do not today, is that the bread and wine that Jesus empowers the priest to consecrate during mass, are the outward forms (look, taste, feel, etc.) of the bread and wine. These outward forms, or "accidents", do not change, but their substance or essence does. Jesus knew this teaching would be difficult and that many of his disciples would leave him because of it. However, he does not back down and say, "shucks guys I was only talking symbolically, you don't really need to eat my body and blood." He reinforces and repeats the point. Later in John chapter six, he tells his apostles, if you think this teaching is hard to accept, what if I were to tell you that the Son of God would be crucified and then rise from the dead and ascend into heaven??? So, he was sort of saying to them….and to us, "hang in there man, you ain't seen nothing yet"! Please excuse my vernacular!

This begins to give us a little better idea of the omnipotent nature of God. Also, Jesus was reminding us that if we doubt his ability to change the substance of bread and wine into his body and blood, consider he was the same supreme being who made the entire universe with all its complexity and wonder, who created all the species of animals and plants, made man and yes, humbled himself by becoming man to redeem us from our sins. He let us kill him, only to rise from the dead and ascend back into heaven.

How can we can believe in a God who created the whole world, but have trouble believing he can empower priests to transubstantiate bread and wine into his precious body and blood?? However, it still takes faith to believe in the "Real Presence of the Eucharist". I believe it is much easier to accept this dogma when you consider the faith that is required to believe in God, or to believe that every time a new baby is conceived, it is made in God's image via the soul it receives from God the Father thru the Holy Spirit. This miracle happens many times each day, just like the miracle of transubstantiation.

69. When the priests pour the water into the wine at mass, what does that symbolize?

I must admit, I had never really given this much thought until your question. However, the origin of this practice dates back to the ancient world. In the Jewish world, wine was drunk "straight up", but in the early Grecian world they tended to "cut" their wine with water. The Greeks added water to wine because it was often thick, gritty, and too strong. It was simply good taste to add water to wine before drinking it. The Romans loved all things Greek, so they adopted Greek manners and spread them to the lands they conquered. And even though it was not originally a Jewish custom to add water to wine, it soon became part of the Passover meal itself and, hence, part of our Mass. As the celebration of the Eucharist moved from its roots in Palestine to the surrounding Roman world, the Roman practice of cutting the wine with water naturally became part of the celebration.

As early as the fourth century, catechists explained that the water represented humanity and the wine, divinity. Once you put the water into the wine, it's impossible to take it out again. Because of Jesus, humanity can never again be separated permanently from God. So, the custom continues. So today, the words the priest says as he pours the water into the wine are, "By the mystery of this water and wine, may we come to share in the divinity of Christ, who humbled himself to share in our humanity." So, the wine was seen as symbolizing Christ's divinity, and the water his humanity.

70. Why does it seem like it was Eve who tempted Adam in the Garden of Eden?

The short answer is that while Adam appears to blame Eve for his sinful act, in reality, he blamed God. Adam said to God, "The woman whom You gave to be with me, she gave me from the tree, and I ate" (Ge 3;12). Don't let the facts get in the way of a good story and keep you from understanding God's intended message. This portion of Genesis was a story intended to deliver a set of messages. One is that we are human, have free wills and may not always exercise those free wills in the best way. We will mess up and sin! The devil is the root of all evil, and regardless of the method or the instrument he uses, he will be constantly working to draw us away from God. He will use your friends, television, movies, and our own weaknesses to tempt us to sin.

So, while in the story of creation it appears that Adam was just an innocent bystander and that Eve led him astray, remember Adam had been told directly by God not to eat of the fruit of this tree and he had his own free will to obey this command or not and he freely chose not to do so. Adam ends up blaming God for his sin. As human beings we tend to blame others rather than to admit we messed up!

Vincent J. Heaton Jr.

71. How do you know what you are destined to do on earth?

Excellent question! I think what you are asking is how do we know if we are following God's will for us or if we are simply ignoring his will and doing what we want to do? There is no easy way to know so therefore we need to constantly work on developing or deepening our relationship with Jesus. We should talk to him like we would to any other close friend.

You should pray regularly and ask God to help you see and know his plan for you. I liken it to knowing if, and when, you should get married to someone. By working hard at a relationship, talking with each other about big and little things, listening to each other you gradually find out if the person you are seeing is right for you. The more time you spend with them the more you get to know them, and it will either feel right or not. There is no sure thing and you may start out feeling you are going down a path that is right for you but as your journey continues it will either continue to feel right or it might not. When things don't feel right, or they feel forced, you should pray more and take advantage of the sacraments which give you more strength, more sanctifying grace. This will help you think things through more clearly.

Therefore, I encourage all of you to pray more and to plan on going on retreats throughout your lives. I pray that each of you someday go on a Cursillo retreat. I have been on numerous retreats but my Cursillo retreat was a real game changer for me spiritually speaking. It is hard to hear and remain fully open to God's plan for us, in our hectic daily grinds with school, sports, cell phones, TV, movies, magazines, peers, parents, friends, using words, ads, phone calls, e-mails, text messages, etc. to bombard you with hundreds of messages a day. We need to find some quiet time, every day, just to clear our heads, stop the noise and just talk to God.

72. Why do Catholics pray to saints or to Mary instead of going straight to *Jesus*?

Catholics pray to Mary and the saints to intercede on their behalf and pray in communion with them. Persons of other faiths will argue that we should only pray to God, or to one of the three persons in God. Why go through a middleman, only God can hear and answer our prayers they will say? They also falsely believe Catholics are worshipping these saints, putting them on an equal level with God. This is not the case. The Church encourages us to pray to the saints, to the dead (who we expect are in heaven with God, part of the "Communion of Saints") and especially to Mary.

We pray to them to intercede on our behalf. We also acknowledge their unique qualities that led to them being canonized as saints. We are not putting them ahead of or equal to God. We believe they are in heaven and can act as our advocates, our intercessors with God. Also, many find it easier to pray to a saint who was human like us and may have led a life that we can relate to and can therefore more readily pray to them to intercede on our behalf.

We are praying in communion with them as often they are asking Jesus for many of the same things that we are praying for like peace, health, and even for the very same people. We are asking them to intercede for us. We are asking them to ask God to answer our prayers We are not praying to them to answer are prayers directly. This is especially true and important when we pray to Mary. We know by the example of the miracle of the Wedding feast of Cana that Jesus will not say no to his mother. Mary and the saints are all like us, they are human and are part of the body of Christ. As we are all part of the same body, we all should work in harmony and support each other, for it is always better for the whole body, to work for the well-being of one of the parts. We are not worshipping Mary or the saints, we are honoring them and seeking their help.

One of my favorite prayers is the *Memorare* where we ask Mary to intercede for us. There is a line at the end that goes, "hear and answer us, amen". However, this is all based on her intercession on our behalf with her son

Jesus. We are not asking or expecting Mary (or any other saint we pray "to" and with) to directly answer our prayer. Remember Jesus said, "knock and the door shall be open to you." By praying both directly to God and through intercessors like the dead, the saints and Mary, we have that many more people, "knocking" on our behalf.

73. Why is everyone born with sin?

Actually, "everyone" was not born with sin, even though some will point to places in the Bible that say ALL men were born with sin. In this case "all" or the Aramaic, Hebrew or Greek equivalent words, were not intended to be taken one hundred percent literally. Did you ever hear someone say something like, "man what a great party, everyone was there", or, "the whole town came out to see the Wheaton North/South game", or, "there were billions of people at the fireworks show downtown"? These are all expressions or words used to convey a message but are not intended to be taken one hundred percent literally. So, while Jesus may have said, "all men were born with sin" he did not mean this one hundred percent literally. Jesus was both God and man and he was born without sin. Adam and Eve, or the first man and woman were born without sin. And, as Catholics, we believe Mary was Immaculately Conceived or born without sin and remained sinless for her entire life.

All the rest of us were born with sin because of the sin committed by Adam and Eve. Because we are human beings created by God with a free will and an intellect, we have the power to choose to do good or evil. Had Adam and Eve not been the first to sin, certainly one of their descendants would have. Therefore, it does not matter if we believe it was Adam or Eve that committed the first sin. The intended message is that as humans we have the intellect to know right from wrong and the freedom to make choices, but we will not always make the right choice. The first time this was done, man separated himself from God and Jesus, God the Son, had to restore that communion.

74. Are we Catholic Christians, Christians, or just Catholic?

Yes! Sorry I could not resist this very short answer. Now let me give you my more typical long-winded answer.

So, if you are a practicing Catholic (that is, you accept all that being a Catholic requires, remember, it is not like the cafeteria at school, we cannot pick only those Catholic Church teachings we like and pass on the ones we find difficult or don't like at all) then, you are also a Christian. Saying you are a Catholic Christian is not inaccurate but is arguably overly specific. All Catholics are Christians, but all Christians are not Catholic. A Christian is someone who believes Jesus is the Christ, the Messiah, and one who follows Jesus's teachings. So, by this definition Catholics are Christians. However, as you may recall, because of the Reformation started by Martin Luther, there are many Christians who do not believe what we as Catholics believe. We have covered many of the key differences over the last several weeks. Some of the dogmas we as Catholics subscribe to that other Christian faiths do not subscribe to, are, but are not limited to: the Real Presence of Christ in the Eucharist; that Peter and his papal successors were appointed to be the head of the Church; that in matters of faith and morals, the pope can establish infallible positions (speak without error); that Mary was Immaculately Conceived, that is, was born without the stain of Original Sin (and remained sinless); that Mary conceived and gave birth to Jesus while remaining a virgin; that Mary was assumed into heaven body and soul shortly after her death; that there is a purification process known as Purgatory; that we have souls that are immortal and are what makes us "in God's image and likeness"; that it is very appropriate to pray to Mary and the saints to intercede on our behalf with Jesus; just to name the major ones. There are various Christian faiths that believe in things or practice things that we do not accept as Catholics. For example, we do not subscribe to the two main protestant doctrines of "sola fide" and "sola scriptura" by faith alone, or by scripture alone respectively. We believe it does matter what you believe, not just that you believe, and that believing is not enough that you must act on your beliefs, do corporal and spiritual works of mercy, etc.

Jesus gave us the Beatitudes for a reason, simply following the Commandments is not enough! We also rely on the Pope and the Magisterium, since they are inspired by the Holy Spirit, to help us interpret and to help us apply God's intended messages contained in Sacred Scripture or as communicated by the Son of God, Jesus, to the ever-changing world in which we live. We do not believe we should be free to totally derive our own beliefs and interpretations and keep or retain portions of Sacred Scripture as we see fit and appropriate, as the doctrine of sola scriptura suggests.

Okay I guess maybe I should have just left the answer at Yes! Once I get started it is hard for me to stop!!

75. When Moses goes to ask the Pharaoh to "let his people go", why does God harden the Pharaoh's heart? Wouldn't he want his followers to be freed and avoid the plagues?

This answer is my own personal belief as I could not find any definitive Catholic teachings that relate specifically to your question, but see what you think? I believe God was using the stubbornness of the Pharaoh as a vehicle to show his supremacy over the 'gods" of the Egyptians and to reveal his divine nature and ability. Also, essentially the plagues were a nuisance (not counting the last most severe plague) and a real problem to the Egyptians and not to their Hebrew slaves, the Israelites, God's chosen people. Everything written in scripture, which was inspired by God, about either God in the Old Testament or Jesus in the New Testament was written for a purpose. More importantly, all the prophecies, acts and teachings that were written about, were performed not just for the people at that time, but for people of all generations and of all cultures. Jesus used nature and other means to demonstrate his divine power to help convey his messages and to clarify his will. There are references in the gospels saying not all of Jesus's actions or words were recorded in scripture but those that were recorded are necessary for our salvation. This reinforces for us how important every word is that was included in the Bible.

76. Since Mary was assumed into heaven shortly after her death does that mean she will be live for eternity in heaven?

As confirmed in Father John Hardon's, *The Question and Answer Catholic Catechism,* Mary did in fact die but shortly after her death, her body and soul were reunited and assumed body and soul into heaven. Her body is preserved in spotless chastity; and she shares in her son's redemptive work throughout the world. So yes, she will live in eternity in heaven.

77. If Jesus was omniscient, why did he first say, it was not time for him to start his public life at the wedding feast of Cana if he already knew he was going to do it?

Did you ever hear of having a straight man in a comedy duo or a plant in the audience at a political event to create a forum for the candidate to make points he/she wants to make? Well, without trivializing the miracle and four key messages of this awesome biblical story, this is kind of what Jesus was doing. It was no accident that Jesus "selected" this venue and time to perform his first miracle.

Jesus used only three of his thirty-three years on earth to reveal himself and to publicly preach and create a new law and a new relationship with his people. In a subtle way he was showing that as God, he needed a relatively short time to conquer sin and death and open the gates of heaven.

To your specific question, Jesus was using this objection to his mother's request to demonstrate to us that he, even as the Son of God, will not refuse a request from his mother. This is an invitation to us to pray to Mary, for her to intercede on our behalf. It is also a promise to us that he will answer any petition Mary asks him to address. Be careful here, this does not mean Jesus will answer the petitions Mary requests of him exactly the WAY we want him to (remember Mary did not tell Jesus how to solve the bride's mother's request for help with the wine) or WHEN we want him to. We must be open to God's will, to his plan for us, and for the others for whom we pray.

His other messages were to reinforce the sanctity and importance of his covenant or his promise to his people by performing his first miracle at a wedding, a covenant between a man and a woman. Remember he will later change the Old Testament law that allowed divorce and remarriage to reinforce that what God joins, man may not separate.

It also was no accident that his first miracle was to turn water into wine. He was preparing us for an even greater miracle when he would institute the Sacrament of the Holy Eucharist at the Last Supper and turn wine into His Precious Blood and bread into His Sacred Body. He then gave his disciples and all their priestly successors the authority and power to repeat this miracle of turning wine and bread into his blood and body at every single mass all over the world until the Final Judgement Day.

78. Didn't Elizabeth conceive a son John at and age well beyond child-bearing years? Why is he not held in such high regard and looked upon as God the Father's son Jesus?

Let me clarify a few points. Elizabeth was Mary's cousin and she conceived John the Baptist approximately six months prior to Mary's conception of Jesus. You are correct, it was a miraculous pregnancy as Elizabeth was very old and well beyond childbearing years, yet God had promised Elizabeth she would bear a child, a very important one. His promise was fulfilled BUT not in the same way that Mary was able to conceive and bear a child. Mary was a virgin and conceived a child because the Holy Spirit overshadowed her. Thus, Mary became the bride of the Holy Spirit and the mother of the Son of God, Jesus. Jesus was/is both fully divine and fully human. Elizabeth became pregnant through normal means through her husband Zechariah and gave birth to a fully human boy we now know as

John the Baptist. You should read more on this if you want to know how the child came to be named "John".

So, while we do in fact, greatly celebrate the importance of John the Baptist's role in preparing the way for Jesus, we naturally do not place him as an equal to Jesus nor do we place his mother anywhere near equal to that of Mary. Remember, contrary to the practices of the time when a younger person meets, and older person and the younger person shows respect (obeisance) to the older person in a formal greeting, it was the older Elizabeth who shows respect for the much younger Mary by saying "Hail Mary perfected in grace".

79. Why did God send Jesus down from heaven? Why that time period? What would have happened if he came during a different time period. What is Jesus's last name?

God sent his only Son to become man to both conquer original sin/death, so the gates of heaven could be reopened to us and to change/expand his relationship with his people. Many forget this second reason. God was possibly feared more than he was loved back in the Old Testament times despite all the good God did for his people. But remember "Fear of the Lord" is one of the seven gifts of the Holy Spirit. While you could substitute the word "awe' for "fear", it is healthy to have a proper "fear" of God or respect for his all-powerful nature.

Examples of this permeate the entire Old Testament and in particular, in the Book of Exodus. The Egyptians learned about "Fear of the Lord" the hard way through the various plagues and the Israelites did as well by virtue of the fact that they were left to "wander in the desert" for forty years as punishment for the multiple times they turned against the Lord.

In the New Testament we see how Jesus builds on the Ten Commandments given to us through Moses in the Old Testament, by giving us the Beatitudes and teaching us how to pray. The Ten Commandments are more about things we SHALL NOT DO but Jesus wanted us to also think about things we SHOULD DO. Therefore, he gave us the eight Beatitudes, and therefore we believe as Catholics, it is not enough just to believe or to have faith, but to actively live your faith. The service projects you are working on as part of your preparation for the Sacrament of Confirmation are a reminder of this and hopefully will become a part of your everyday life, not just for a few months while you prepare for this sacrament.

We do not know why God decided to become incarnate (take on a human nature) when he did, where he did, and as he did, as a male Nazarene. Had he come at a very different time and in a very different place (maybe even here in the United States) his message and overall approach would arguably have been the same. I used to think that if Jesus had delayed his coming to our present day, maybe he would have selected women disciples and thus we would have had women priests. I used to think Jesus only selected male disciples back when he came because women were treated as inferiors and so he only selected males because a woman would not have been a credible disciple back then.

It was pointed out to me by my local parish priest that everything Jesus did when he was on earth bucked tradition and went against established authority and practice. He hung out with sinners, he defied the pharisees, he stood up to Roman authorities and he banned divorce and remarriage, to name only a few examples. He was not trying to "fit in" or conform to local practices. Furthermore, he was God, he could have done whatever he wanted, regardless of what was "normal" or traditional at the time. So, it does follow that if God wanted women priests, he would have had women disciples...regardless of when and where he became man.

Jesus, like others of his time did not have formal last names like we do. They often were tied to an occupation to like Joseph, the carpenter or John the black smith. Also, one would be referred as the son or daughter of someone. Eventually, last names were formed. This is one reason why we have many last names today that are derived from occupations (Carpenter, Smith, Shepherd, etc.).

80. What is the most important commandment, and why?

I did not even have to research this question for both of your questions were asked of Jesus when he was preaching on the hillsides of Jerusalem. I will not presume to be able to give a better answer than he provided.

So instead of picking one of the ten original commandments when asked the same first question, "which commandment is the greatest?", Jesus instituted a new "Great Commandment". This was and is, "You shall love the Lord your God, with all your heart, with all your being, with all your strength, and with all your mind, and your neighbor as yourself" (Lk 10:27). So why did he give us a new commandment and why is this the most important or greatest you ask?

Think about what Jesus wanted to accomplish when he became man, when he, the Word, became flesh and dwelt among us. Many correctly say he came down to open the gates of heaven, to fulfill the Old Testament prophecy to conquer sin and death. However, that was not all he looked to accomplish. He wanted to totally change the relationship he had with his people and fulfill other prophecies such as instituting a new law or a new order. God's relationship with his people in the Old Testament was more one of, "Fear of the Lord" rather than "Love of the Lord". By becoming man, Jesus wanted to have his people act not out of fear but act out of love. Therefore, he gave us the Beatitudes.

The Beatitudes are teachings on how we are to live our lives. While he retained the Ten Commandments, which cover more things we "should not do", he wanted to balance these with things we "should do". This further argues against the protestant doctrine of "sola fide" by faith alone. Jesus taught us through the Beatitudes that believing is not enough. He was telling us we will be saved by both believing and acting on these beliefs, living our lives', accordingly, doing kind acts for others in our community.

So, he re-emphasized this by giving us a new "Great Commandment". There are two parts to this new commandment, to this new order. Re-read it! If you consistently and thoroughly follow the two parts of this Great Commandment you will also be following all other Ten Commandments. Actually, later on, Jesus adds another spin on this Great Commandment. He essentially builds on it, clarifies the second part of this new commandment. He clarifies the depth of seriousness to which we should take this commandment. He tells us, "Love one another. As I have loved you, so you must love one another" (Jn 13:34).

This is very hard to do with consistency in our everyday lives but the more fully we treat all we meet or interact with (for me it is how I treat other drivers on the road) as Jesus taught us by his own example, the more closely we will be getting to perfection. It is much easier to love those that are being good to us, or to love them as Jesus would, that are more like us; that hold the same religious, political or moral beliefs that we do; or, those that we know very well. Much harder to love those that are very different from us, are mean to us, or do not behave as we would like. Therefore, this Great Commandment is the greatest or most important commandment of all!

81. Why does God not come down to help us?

He already did! I was tempted to leave it here but...did not want to come off the wrong way. So, he accomplished all he needed to in his three short years on earth. However, he is always with us. He is all around you, with you, and is always there for you. All we need do is "knock" and the door will be opened. Sometimes he may be slower getting to the door or even if he was physically here, he might still choose to answer your knock differently than you would like. He left us seven sacraments, he taught us how to pray, and he promised us he would always be with us. We need to pray, to develop a close relationship with him by always talking to him and by learning more about our faith. We receive grace (help) through prayer, participation in mass, and through the other sacraments that are open to us. God is with us in a very special very real way in the Holy Eucharist.

What a great gift this is and what an opportunity to be in full communion with him (pun intended!)

Our challenge is to understand God's will or plan for us, or for others whom we love, and for whom we may be praying, may be different than our wills, wants and expectations. We also need to appreciate his timetable may be different than ours. Some believe God is not listening or responding because he is not giving us what WE want, when WE want it. He always listens, hears and then responds. We may be the ones that are not hearing or responding.

Friendships take work, sacrifice, dialog and love. It is no different in our relationship with God. He made the ultimate sacrifice and shows us his love by being such a forgiving God. We need to maintain the dialog and constantly seek out his help!

82. How can people believe in someone they cannot see? What keeps you strong in your faith?

So, first let me ask you, have you lost a close relative or friend to death? You guys are younger (by a factor) so you may not have had to deal with this, but I am sure you know people who have. We still remember all the good these people did, the positive influence they had on the lives they touched, and we pray for them, and to them, to help us. They were there and now they are not.

Yes, it is harder to relate to someone you never personally met and cannot see. Jesus tried to help us with this concept by using St. Thomas the apostle, as an example. Remember, everything Jesus said and did over his short time of being physically with us was for a purpose. That purpose was not only directed to the people of his time but to each one of us today and those who have yet to be born. It was no accident St. Thomas was not in the locked room where the apostles were hiding after Jesus's crucifixion when he suddenly appeared. Thomas could not believe Jesus rose from the dead and was able to enter the locked room without use of the door.

He said he would not believe until he could put his fingers in Jesus's nail wounds and could place his hand in Jesus's side where he was pierced with the spear. When Jesus appeared again when Thomas was present, he then believed. Jesus, said, "happy are those who have not seen, yet believe." Easy to say but hard to do.

We must have faith but, I think the key lies in the answer to your second question, "What keeps you strong in your faith?" So, believing in someone you have never met and cannot see is very challenging. However, God left us several gifts. One is first the gift of faith, no matter how small that gift is (maybe as small as a mustard seed). He then gave us other gifts to grow that seed of faith if we exercise our free will (another gift of his) to do so. This is a gift of intellect. So, we grow and strengthen our gift of faith through reading, listening and learning about our faith. Every tenet or aspect of our faith has a foundation in logic, philosophy, scripture and church tradition.

The proof God is real is all around us in creation and in each other. God does not have a face or a body. God the Son did take on human form (as Jesus) to overcome the stranglehold of original sin and to open the gates of heaven. Even then he did not show his face (we saw the human face of Jesus; his divine essence is not something we can see or identify with any of our human senses) nor did this provide physical proof God existed. The only time we know God revealed his divine glory was on the mountain to a few of his disciples, Peter, James and John. The brightness of his glory and divinity was so bright they could not look directly at him. God is a supreme being and cannot be defined or limited by human beings' realities (We keep trying to understand and explain divine nature in terms of our human natures or limits of our human experience).

I have challenged each of you to ask hard questions about your faith, not to cause doubt, but to get you to think, to exercise your intellects and to encourage you to want to learn more. Knowledge is power! The more you know about your faith and its foundation, the easier it will be for you to become comfortable with it, to believe in it, strengthen it and effectively share it with others. Other ways to strengthen your faith and relationship with Jesus are through prayer, participation in the sacraments and by reading Sacred Scripture.

83. Why was Mary born without sin?

The short answer is Mary was to be the means or the vessel by which the Son of God, Jesus, our Lord and Savior was to be brought into the world. So, this is a matter of faith but consider also the logic. By example, if you were going to bring a rare, ancient fragile document across the world and present it as a gift to a foreign leader and his people, would you not carry the document in a strong safe and clean vessel or box?? You would not want anything to harm it, dirty it or minimize its chances of getting there safely and being a gift fitting a king or president.

This is what happened first in the Old Testament when they traveled with the sacred scrolls which contained the Word, or God's message in writing to us. They carried it in a sacred box called the Ark of the Covenant. Only the high priest could touch this very specifically and specially designed and crafted box. It was kept clean and pristine.

Now in the New Testament we have God becoming man or the Word becoming flesh. God was not going to take any chances that this gift to us and his mission would be compromised by delivering it to us through an unclean, weak or vulnerable vessel or person. Mary and her womb needed to be the perfect vessel and one that would remain so to be the strong Mother she needed to be to bring Jesus safely into the world and to raise him properly. For this reason, to be the perfect vessel, she needed to be born without sin and remain sinless.

There were only four "people" born without sin, Adam, Eve, Mary and Jesus. Only two of these people never sinned at all in their lives, Jesus and Mary. Jesus is God the Son and Mary, the Mother of our Lord, was the New Testament fulfillment of Eve and of the Ark of the Covenant. Many Old Testament persons and things have New Testament counterparts that fulfill and supplant them. When this occurs, the New Testament counterpart is always superior in nature and/or in position to the Old Testament person or object it fulfills or supplants.

Mary is the superior New Testament fulfillment of Eve. Eve, while born without sin, eventually commits the first sin and arguably others after the big first one. Mary was born without sin as well and is understood to have remained sinless throughout her life. The *Catechism of the Catholic Church* tells us, "Mary benefitted first of all and uniquely from Christ's victory over sin: she was preserved from all stain of original sin and by a special grace from God committed no sin of any kind during her whole earthly life" (CCC 411).

So, you can see that on multiple levels that Mary is the New Testament superior to both Eve and the Ark of the Covenant and that there is a good foundation for believing Mary was Immaculately Conceived and remained sinless. This is further supported by infallible Papal decree that addresses these aspects of Mary and her Assumption body and soul into heaven. Read Father Harden's, *The Question and Answer Catholic Catechism,* (pages 65-71) if you want more insight.

84. What is the difference between the Catholic Church and a Trinity Church.

As Catholics we do believe there is one God, that Jesus is the Son of God made man, that he was crucified died and was buried and then rose from the dead to conquer sin and death, and that he established one Church on earth with Peter at its head as the first Pope. There are many different religions, including many thousands of Christian denominations (those that believe Jesus was the Son of God but differ with Catholics in many other areas) and many other non-Christian religions. Some religions recognize other entities as god's (Allah, Buddha, animals, the sun, etc.).

If you were born to Muslim parents instead of Catholic parents, you might very well be Muslim today. Many have never been exposed to or heard the teachings of Jesus Christ and those of the Catholic Church. They never had a chance to compare their religion to Catholicism and make an informed faith-based decision. It is for this reason I have encouraged you to ask questions about your faith, not to cause you to doubt your faith or weaken your resolve, but to help you better understand WHAT we believe as Catholics and WHY we hold these beliefs. Hopefully this will not only strengthen your faith but will help you defend it and win over others.

This is all part of preparing yourself for Confirmation so when you tell the bishop on the night of your Confirmation that you "believe" (and as you recite the Creed at mass) you will know what you are saying you believe about your faith. Some of the strongest, most articulate Catholics we have are those that converted from another faith. They typically have researched, studied and prayed harder and understand better the specifics behind the Catholic Church's dogma and its teachings and positions than most who were raised as Catholics from childhood. They have had a chance to see the Catholic faith from a different perspective which is very healthy.

Everyone can be happy with God in heaven, whether they "knew" him on earth or not and regardless of what religious denomination they lived their lives under. The *Catechism of the Catholic Church* reminds us:

> "Since Christ died for all, and since all men are called to one and the same destiny, which is divine, we must hold that the Holy Spirit offers to all the possibility of being made partakers, in a way known to God, of the paschal mystery." Every man who is ignorant of the Gospel of Christ and of his church but seeks the truth and does the will of God in accordance with his understanding of it, can be saved. It may be supposed that such persons would have *desired Baptism explicitly* if they had known its necessity" (CCC 1260).

This means that as long as we are in communion with the God we know, the God that loves us, and return that love, we can receive sanctifying grace. Just living a good moral life and being a "good" person is not sufficient. We need to respond to our God's love in a real and tangible way.

Those who know and Jesus can take comfort in his most forgiving and merciful nature. Jesus forgave those that crucified him as they were torturing him and forcing him to succumb to the worst form of death possible at the time. We believe as Catholics that it is not enough to simply believe in Jesus but that we live what we believe through our words and actions. Many Christian religions believe it is "enough" to simply accept Jesus as their Lord and Savior and that it does not matter how they live their life or what they believe in. However, I find it hard for someone to say they have fully accepted Jesus and then not live their lives' accordingly. Jesus said, "I give you a new commandment: love one another, as I have loved you, so you also should love one another" (Jn 13/34).

85. Why did Jesus use figurative forms of speech or teaching?

Jesus used parables or stories that were based in typical everyday type events or situations to deliver specific messages and he used simple terminology to tell those stories. He used this approach for several reasons. First and foremost, the people he preached to at the time largely lacked any formal education and lived rather simple lives (certainly compared to today's standards) as they were primarily, shepherds, fishermen, farmers, etc. He had to speak in ways they could understand and in ways they could easily remember and pass on. Stories or parables can be easily listened to, told and retold without losing their basic meaning. People find stories easier to listen to and since they related to their own lives, could see themselves as Jesus intended, as being part of the very message or story Jesus was telling.

Whenever Jesus delivered a message through his parabolic preaching's, he always knew if they were grasping his point or if they were confused, uncertain, or disturbed by it. Since Jesus was all knowing, or omniscient, he knew if he had to re-tell the story or reinforce the story with additional teachings to get his point across. Jesus knew when he challenged the people and even his own disciples, to accept the very difficult message of the need to eat his body and drink his blood to have eternal life, that this would be difficult for them. He knew they were not all getting his real meaning and he knew he would lose many followers as a result but that did not deter him from his mission or from communicating what he wanted the people of his time and us to hear and believe.

Whenever Jesus spoke, and certainly whatever the inspired writers of scripture wrote about his teachings and his works, they were done not just for the people around at that time but for all generations to follow. He had to preach in Aramaic, the language of his time and place, but in a way that would not lose its core meaning thousands of years later when you or I heard or read those stories. This was even more difficult given how many different translations and transliterations his literal words would go through over time and how different the world would be at varying points in time and in varying places across the globe.

I believe Jesus spoke cryptically at times, on purpose. I believe he wanted to draw people to himself, wanted them to seek him out, to want to get to know him to know him on a personal level. He did not want to force himself on the people of his time, nor on us today.

Some of his messages are difficult to fully comprehend today on our own because we are not as familiar with the cultural and historical situation or circumstances that influenced what he said and how he said it. We are further challenged by the fact that we are reading his messages from an English Bible targeted to certain ages or types of readers. Jesus spoke in Aramaic and his words and actions were first written down in Greek and then in Latin before being translated and transliterated into many other different languages. This can help explain why his messages may seem more subtle or difficult to be sure what he was really trying to communicate to us.

These are only some of the reasons we need to rely on the Pope and the Magisterium (teaching/guiding body) of the Church to help interpret and apply Jesus's intended messages and specific scriptural passages to our current world and culture. Jesus promised Peter, our first Pope, and thus all other Popes to follow, he would be there for him, to guide him and to help him. He then told Peter, "feed my sheep". Another figurative way of saying, I will help you and inspire you, so you can lead and help my people understand my messages and live their lives according to my teachings.

86. Is it wrong not to believe everything the Catholic Church teaches?

So, I am going to answer this good question from the point of view that you are asking this question as a Catholic, not believing or fully accepting all the teachings and dogmas of the Catholic faith.

This is a very sensitive question for there are many that identify as Catholics who do not fully accept and do not follow all the teachings of the Catholic Church. It is one thing to not fully follow all the teachings because in our human nature, we are weak and succumb to peer pressure, to our own selfishness or to the temptations of the devil and we commit sins. We may accept the teaching but then not fully follow them, i.e. we sin. We accept as Catholics that we must keep Holy the Sabbath (go to mass on Sunday/ or Saturday night) but we do not always do so. Some accept the general teaching but don't treat missing Sunday mass as the mortal sin that it is. If we intentionally miss mass, we are obligated to go to confession and get absolution before going to mass and receiving communion again. Many Catholics don't know or don't accept this aspect.

The bigger problem is not accepting key dogmas or teachings of the Catholic Church but then believing we are still Catholic. The Catholic faith does not follow the protestant doctrine of sola fide. That is, as Catholics we do not agree with our protestant friends who say it does not matter what we specifically believe but only that you accept Jesus Christ as our Lord and Savior. One of the key reasons there are so many thousands of different Christian faiths is the doctrine of sola fide, by faith alone. These different Christian denominations vary in their specific beliefs about God's message on how we are to live our lives, but they all accept Jesus was the

Messiah and that he died for our sins. As Catholics we have very specific tenets, dogmas, teachings we accept as part of our faith and we accept there are specific things we must do too live out our Catholic faith.

Some people believe they can be Catholics and still say it is okay or acceptable to have an abortion, or it is okay to get divorced and remarry, to live a homosexual lifestyle, or to do (or not do) many other things the Church says are not consistent with Catholic doctrine. So, you see I am distinguishing between sinning and believing it is okay to behave in ways contrary to Church teachings and still call oneself a Catholic.

A condition for an act to be a sin is that I must know the act is wrong and then of one's own free will, go ahead and commit the wrong act (or omit to do something we should do, like go to mass on Sunday). We all will sin from time to time but can still be Catholic. Of course, we need to regularly go to Reconciliation and work on amending our lives'. This is different from believing it is okay to have an abortion or to have same sex relations, or believe it is okay to regularly miss Sunday mass and still believe you are a practicing Catholic. Many want to pick and choose which teachings of the Catholic Church they want to accept and which ones they can ignore and yet still be considered Catholic. You either are a Catholic or you are not.

Now please know that you may not fully comprehend why the Catholic Church holds the positions it does or even buy fully into all the related logic. However, as long as you live your life in a manner consistent with Catholic Church teachings you remain Catholic. However, you have an obligation to know what the Catholic Church teaches and why, and to pray to God for help to better understand and accept these Articles of Faith as part of your own beliefs and to live your life accordingly.

87. Why do people go to hell if Jesus/God forgives all of us?

While Jesus is most forgiving, for remember he forgave those who were crucifying him as they were in the process of doing so, it does not mean, and the Church does not profess, that all who sin will be forgiven and be welcomed into heaven. We do not know the full extent of Jesus's forgiving nature or where he draws the line. For this reason, it is important to live our lives as best we can and when we do stumble and commit venial sins and certainly if we commit mortal sins, to repent, go to the Sacrament of Reconciliation, seek absolution and work on amending our past sinful ways. Those that go to hell will be those who have totally rejected Jesus or have totally lived their lives in a way that rejected all that is good and consciously chose evil over good. So, these people that totally reject God, that totally reject good and opt for evil, are condemning themselves to hell. They have chosen hell by rejecting God. I am not including those who commit evil acts but are not of sound mind or those who have been very evil in their lives but then truly repent. Here we rely on God's most forgiving nature. I am very glad I will be judged by God and not by a "jury of my peers".

88. What means most to God:

1. **Praying;**
2. **Acting and portraying a good Christian life (living the Ten Commandments); or,**
3. **Believing in God and Jesus as our Lord Savior?**

All of these are important. Praying, your first option, provides sanctifying grace; and, praying is a necessary part of any good Christian's or Catholic's life in cultivating a personal relationship with Christ. However, like option number three, it cannot be your only path to heaven. I suppose if one prayed very frequently, that same person is probably not out committing grievous sins against their fellow man and against God. However, if the prayer is occasional and is brought on only with a view to cover the bases "just in case" there is a God, a heaven and a hell, etc., following the commission of sinful deeds, or only to ask for help in very difficult times or times of want or need, then this is quite another matter.

Of course, belief in God and Jesus as the Son of God, your third option is very important but sounds too much like many protestant denominations' belief in "sola fide", that is, "by faith alone". This protestant doctrine suggests the specifics of what you believe, or how you live your life, does not really matter, it requires only that you believe and accept Jesus as your Lord and Savior. As Catholics, we believe this is far too passive a doctrine and misses several key aspects of living a good Catholic or Christian life. Under some interpretations of the doctrine of sola fide, you could live a selfish life of caring only for yourself, you could be cruel to your fellow man, not be a good spouse or parent, and live basically a sinful life, just as long as you "believed" and accepted Jesus as your savior. In fact, many believe the Lord is so forgiving that they can live a very self-centered or even sinful life and still get to heaven. All they need to do is believe in God.

Jesus taught us we must not only believe but that we must act on these beliefs and it is our actions, coupled with our faith that lead to salvation (or not). Jesus said that the gate to heaven is narrow and not all will have the strength to pass through. This statement clearly states eternal salvation requires effort. This message is reinforced by Jesus through the Parables of the Ten Virgins and the Parable of the Talents. In both these parables, ALL the subjects believed, but some acted on their beliefs very differently from their peers. As such, some were invited into the feast or were honored (both synonymous with being invited into heaven) while others were not (synonymous with being sent to hell). The five unprepared virgins believed the Groom (Jesus) was coming but did not have sufficient oil (they did not act properly and the one servant in the parable of the talents, for fear of doing the wrong thing, did nothing, despite all of the gifts/abilities he was given by God.

Right after the accounts of these two parables in Matthew's Gospel, the Final Judgement is described as the separation of the sheep on his right and the goats on his left. It was the sheep who fed, clothed and cared for others who were saved. The goats on the left, who knew Jesus (for they called him Lord) but did not extend the same love for their fellow man, who did not try to love others as Jesus taught us by his own example, who were not saved.

Now please note, I believe way too much is made of this debate over this whole topic between fundamental Christians and Catholics on being saved by faith alone. Most Christians who profess to have accepted Jesus Christ as their Lord and Savior, live their lives' accordingly through their regular thoughts, words and actions. If one truly accepts Jesus Christ as their Lord and Savior then they are also accepting Jesus for who he said he was, the example he gave us, the messages he conveyed and pattern their daily lives accordingly…to the best of their ability.

So, I trust you can now see why your option number two was more appealing to me but also, I saw very little difference between options two and three. However, I would add one caveat or clarification to option two as worded. This option implied that by living a good Christian life, you even said "acting", one would get to heaven. I agree but feel compelled to comment on your clarification.

In parentheses you seemed to stipulate that "acting" as a good Christian or Catholic was defined by following the Ten Commandments. I agree, but also suggest that, according to Jesus, this is not enough! Again, you ask, "Why?" Well, when Jesus became man and spoke to the people on the mountain side, he gave us an additional challenge. He gave us the eight Beatitudes. The Beatitudes were Jesus's teachings on how we should live our lives, on things that we should be doing on a daily basis. The Ten Commandments are important, but they are primarily focused on things we should not do. Jesus was being very clear to us here. He was telling us we not only have to resist temptation and to refrain from sinning, but that we had to go further. He was instructing us to imitate him, to treat others with the same love and compassion, mercy and forgiveness he showed to those he encountered.

Then what happened next? He gave us a new commandment, the Great Commandment. "You shall love the Lord your God, with all your heart, with all your being, with all your strength, and with all your mind, and love your neighbor as yourself" (Lk 10:27). But then Jesus expanded on the Great Commandment by giving us an even more challenging extension of this commandment, "A new command I give you: Love one another. As I have loved you, so you must love one another" (Jn 13:34). So clearly Jesus was commanding us to imitate his behavior to the very best of our ability!

Finally, I would add, we are the ones who decide or determine our eternal fate. We have free wills to accept Jesus and his way of life or to reject him. Even if we never had opportunity to know Christ, we still have free wills to decide to either live a "good" life, treating others as we would want to be treated, or not. God will ultimately separate those on his right or on his left based on the choices we made throughout our lives', but his decision will be based on our decisions.

89. If God created all of mankind and our universe, then he created gay people. Since he did make each one of us, why is being gay a sin?

There is a flaw in your logic.

First, let me speak to the logic issue. If you take your basic point to its logical extension, then any of us could argue that since God made us, it does not matter how we live our lives…since God made us this way. You imply that since God made us, our decisions do not matter. Now to be fair, I understand you may be stating that being gay is not a decision we make but that we are either born gay or we are not. There are secular and scientific arguments on both sides of this question, but I would argue, and the Catholic Church would as well, that it is really a moot point.

The Church does not teach being gay or having a gay tendency is a sin. The Church does teach that living a homosexual lifestyle, specifically, engaging in same sex relations is a sin. A person with gay tendencies may not act on those tendencies. It is not sinful for two gay or homosexual persons to live together, provided they do not interact sexually.

God created all men (and women, of course) and yet some exercise their free wills and become drug addicts, alcoholics, obese, as well as robbers, murderers, rapists, etc. Your logic implies that since God made them, their selected lifestyles or behaviors should not be sinful. God did make us all and he also gave us, unlike any other of his creations, intellects and free wills. We have the power to decide how we will live our lives and yes, to decide to sin or not.

The Catholic Church has many positions regarding sexual behavior that are not popular in today's world for other Christian faiths and for many Catholics. These include, in addition to condoning only heterosexual relationships, the Church's position against abortion, against the use of contraceptives, and the inability to remarry following divorce if the former spouse is alive, and many other positions.

While a person may have a desire or a proclivity to engage in same sex relations, just like a heterosexual person may have a desire to engage in pre-marital sexual relations or a married person may want to have sexual relations with persons other than their spouse, the Church considers this sinful. Likewise, to indulge to an excess in other areas of our lives could also be sinful. We are obligated to control our desires to exercise our free wills consistent with the Ten Commandments and the teachings of the Catholic Church.

So, if the question then is, why does the church believe same sex relations are sinful you need to go to the *Catechism of the Catholic Church* for details on this topic. You should read the entire section covering *Article Six, The Sixth Commandment* (CCC 2331-2391) but there are other great Catholic books/resources that cover this and related aspects of this topic in depth. You need to be sure you are reading texts that are totally consistent with the Catholic Church and Holy See teachings. The short, high-level answer is that since same sex relations cannot lead to procreation, the conception of a child, they are disordered and sinful. The Church, for similar and other activity specific reasons, holds that lust, masturbation, fornication, pornography, prostitution and rape are all gravely sinful acts.

90. According to the Bible, when does the world end?

The Bible does not say, nor did Jesus say when the world would end. This is the whole point of the parable of the bride's maids (Mt 25:1-13). The bride's maids were waiting for the groom to arrive and planned to light his way with their oil-based lamps. Half brought extra oil "for they knew not what hour the groom (God) would arrive". The other half had their oil burn out during the early hours of their wait (did not have enough sanctifying grace) and asked if they could borrow some from the others who had extra. But those bridesmaids who had extra responded saying, "we do not know when he will come and want to be sure to be ready to light his way, go into town and get more oil before the groom arrives." Of course, while they were gone the groom arrived and those that were ready were invited into the wedding feast (heaven) while the others were left out (in purgatory or hell). The moral of the story is that we must always be ready for we do not know when we will die nor when the end of the world will be.

However, the end of our earthly, mortal world will come to an end, at least as we know it, on the Final Judgment Day. On this day all of us will either be welcomed to eternal life with God or banished to eternal punishment. This eternal punishment is a state of definitive self-exclusion from communion with God and the blessed, it is called "hell".

91. Why did God create the universe and put us on earth?

God created man, over the other animals and plants, etc. out of love and to enable us to share in his being, his wisdom and his goodness. Or, as I learned, through the *Baltimore Catechism,* God made us to know him, to love him, to serve him (you serve him by serving others, for he said, "whatever you do to the least of my little ones, you do unto me"), and to be happy with him in heaven. So, God created us in his image and likeness and gives us the opportunity to freely live as he showed and instructed us through the Ten Commandments, the Beatitudes and how he treated or loved others. Our ultimate reward will be to join him in eternal happiness in heaven.

The *Catechism of the Catholic Church* answers your question in sections 293-294 by stating:

> Scripture and Tradition never cease to teach and celebrate this fundamental truth: "The world was made for the glory of God." St. Bonaventure explains that God created all things "not to increase his glory but to show it forth and to communicate it," for God has no other reason for creating than his love and goodness: "Creatures came into existence when the key of love opened his hand." The First Vatican Council explains:

> This one, true God, of his own goodness and "almighty power," not for increasing his own beatitude, not for attaining his perfection, but in

> order to manifest this perfection through the benefits he bestows on creatures, with absolute freedom of counsel "and from the beginning of time, made out of nothing, both orders of creatures, the spiritual and the corporeal..."

> The glory of God consists in the realization of this manifestation and communication of his goodness, for which the world was created. God made us "to be his sons through Jesus Christ, according to the purpose of his will, *to the praise of his glorious grace," for* "the glory of God is man fully alive; moreover man's life is the vision of God: if God's revelation through creation has already obtained life for all the beings that dwell on earth, how much more will the Word's manifestation of the Father obtain life for those who see God." The ultimate purpose of creation is that God "who is the creator of all things may at last become 'all in all,' thus simultaneously assuring his own glory and our beatitude."

He did not create us because he had nothing better to do of for his own gratification. He created us so we would have the opportunity to achieve everlasting eternal life with him in heaven. I cannot imagine dealing with a terminal illness or being on my deathbed without the promise of a glorious eternal life ahead.

92. How do we know our religious beliefs are correct?

For the purposes of answering this question I am going to assume you mean the "Roman Catholic Church" when you say "our" religious beliefs. Also, your use of the word "correct" implies that all other beliefs are incorrect. This is not the case. In fact, we have more in common with many other Christian faiths than we have differences. That said, the Roman Catholic Church believes it is the one true church established by Jesus Christ. In fact, Catholic means universal (open to all). However, not all have heard Jesus's word or have had the opportunity to really come to know or understand the teachings of the Catholic faith. Just as you have been raised Catholic, others may have been raised with other religious beliefs. This does not make them all wrong and certainly does not mean those practicing these other faith denominations won't get to heaven.

However, it does not make sense God the Father would: send his Son to earth; become incarnate; establish his kingdom here on earth; allow us to torture and crucify him; and then, upon his Resurrection and Ascension; leave us to our own devices! He would not have had much divine foresight if he had not left a structure behind to help ensure the continuity of the Church he established to fulfill his promise that the "gates of hell shall not prevail against the Church". He knew our world would evolve and change overtime and would need help applying his unchanging message to this everchanging world let alone the help each of us would need to apply his message and teachings to our own personal lives. He understood that his message would not always be easy to comprehend or to accept. For this reason, he made Peter the head of the Church and promised him the grace and power of the Holy Spirit to ensure his Church would never die and to help him infallibly interpret and communicate his message.

As I mentioned earlier, there are over 26,000 different Christian religious denominations. Most of these denominations were formed because individuals did not like one or more of the Church's interpretations of God's truth as it relates to living our lives today. We may not like or even understand some of the Catholic Church's teachings, but we must accept them and live by them to be a Catholic. Therefore, I encourage all of you to learn WHY the Catholic Church holds the dogmatic positions it does. This will help you better understand, accept, communicate, defend and strengthen your faith.

93. Is it okay to watch an R rated movie?

It is not okay if your parents tell you may not see R rated movies or if you know you must first receive permission and you do not. It is also not okay if you know the movie is immoral. We are supposed to "avoid the occasion of sin". This means we are not to do things or go to places that may lead us into temptation or to sin. You must decide what is immoral and what may lead you to sin as you grow older. Just as you should avoid hanging with kids you know will do things you know are wrong or your parents would forbid you to do. So, you should avoid going to movies you believe will be immoral or lead you to sin. Even the movie industry, which has never been accused of being a terribly moral lot, warns you must be seventeen or accompanied by an adult to see an R rated movie.

94. Why is Mary usually shown wearing blue?

Colors have very specific meanings in the church. There are specific reasons for the various vestment colors the priests wear when they say mass and for the colors of the advent wreath candles to name only a couple examples. There are several different answers to this question that I found but I cannot say they are authoritative or that the Church has an authoritative position on your question. Here are two I found.

1. In one religious document the author applied the following meanings to the color blue as it specifically related to Mary: Blue reflects calm, tranquility, purity, divinity, spiritual love, truth, fidelity and constancy. All these seem particularly fitting!

2. You may be interested to know that the great English poet and Jesuit priest, Gerard Manley Hopkins, wrote a poem, *The Blessed Virgin Compared to The Air That We Breathe*. One section of this poem compares the air's blueness to the Virgin's transparent acceptance of God's will: "Blue be it. This blue heaven -- the seven, or seven times seven, hued sunbeam shall transmit per-fect, not alter it. So, God was God of old. A Mother came to mold ...." Perhaps, Hopkins was latching onto something theologically revealing by comparing Mary to the color blue. You see, color psychologists will tell you that of red, blue, yellow and green, blue is the one hue that is both "heteronomous" (passive and allowing of others to perform an action) and "concentric" (looking inward). Mary's response to the guardian angel when it was announced that she was to bear the Divine Lord was heteronomous: "let it be done to me according to thy Word". Her nature was concentric, too. She found meaning not so much from going out of herself to receive the Lord (then she would wear yellow) but from humbling her own soul: "My soul magnifies the Lord and my spirit rejoices in God my savior!" Perhaps the art historians are correct about the shading of the clothes and the light rods, but perhaps there is a theological explanation, too? Hope this helps.

95. Why isn't the Catholic Church open to everyone?

It is open to everyone who wants to belong and can accept the precepts, the teachings and the dogmas that define us as Catholics. This is accomplished by learning what they are, accepting them and becoming a baptized Catholic. Anyone with faith and the willingness to learn and abide by the Church's teachings can indeed be Catholics. No one is excluded. Many choose not to become Catholic due to their upbringing in other religious denominations or exclude themselves for other reasons.

It is not easy to be a true practicing Catholic; it takes faith, effort and self-sacrifice. However, remember Catholics do not have a monopoly on heaven. However, I firmly believe Jesus would not have come down to earth, suffer, allowed himself to be crucified and then ascend into heaven and leave us without a specific direction. He would not have said, "I do not care what you believe in about me, my father, my mother Mary, or what the specifics of my message mean to each new generation.

Our own forefathers had enough foresight to develop a constitution and a form of government to protect the sovereignty of our nation. Jesus surely was at least as wise as our forefathers and as such would have established one true church. Many are called to his church, not all respond, while some are not called at all. However, called or not, fully or partially responsive, or totally unresponsive, we all will have an opportunity to be happy with God in heaven. This too, was part of Jesus's message to us when he died on the cross. How will you respond??

96. Where does the Catholic Church stand on Abortion?

To some this may seem like a slam dunk question but there are many who struggle with this, many who claim to be, or want to remain Catholic yet are pro-abortion. The Church is unquestionably against abortion. The Church maintains that the moment a woman's egg is fertilized (at conception), the resulting fetus, no matter how early it is in its development, is in fact a human life. If you have not gone to the Museum of Science and Industry in Chicago and seen the exhibit on the development of the fetus (unborn child) you should. Look how well formed the fetus is and see how clear, to even the least scientific and untrained eye, the fetus is in fact a human life, and how soon in the development process this is evident. Our own US Government has said it is legal to kill the child/fetus via an abortion all the way up through the twenty-fourth week of its life and the State of New York passed a law allowing abortions, murdering the unborn child, right up to the birth date. Recently the State of Illinois passed similar legislation. This is a travesty in my own personal view, but also in the eyes of the

Catholic Church. Terminating a pregnancy, other than if the mother's life is in imminent danger (which, is today, a medical rarity) is against Catholic Church teaching. There are numerous politicians at the national and state levels who claim to be Catholic and yet are pro-abortion and have voted for these laws that fail to protect the lives of these unborn children. I feel the Church should excommunicate any "Catholic" legislator that votes for these pro-abortion laws and in many cases, they have done just that!

The Church is consistent in its position regarding the sanctity of human life and is also against suicide and euthanasia (termination of life to relieve someone in pain or the killing of people considered to be a burden on society). That said, while the Church is neutral on nations' protecting themselves or coming to the aid of others through the participation in war, if all other channels of resolution have been exhausted (diplomatic attempts, sanctions, etc.). However, the Church is against weapons of mass destruction that indiscriminately kill innocent people or destroy large areas where such an occurrence is a likely outcome. God is the one who gives us life, the Church's position is that this sacred gift of life must be protected.

97. If Jesus is omniscient, he would have known when Mary would come to him and asked him to start his public life, so why wasn't he prepared?

Sometimes I can relate as a teacher, to how Jesus must have felt when the Pharisees tried to trap him. Remember when they asked, "whose laws should we obey Caesar's or God's?" Jesus responded by asking for a Roman coin and upon pointing to the likeness of Caesar, said, "give to Caesar that which is Caesar's and to God that which is God's." See even back then he was espousing the doctrine of separation of church and state while deftly avoiding being trapped.

Please know I am not intending to "diss" this question or earlier ones. It is very American and human, to try to find loopholes, contradictions and exceptions to authoritative positions. I believe this is a good, logical question, not intended to trap but to gain knowledge! I encourage you to continually question, in constructive ways, why the Church teaches what it does or when you say you are a Catholic, that you understand what being Catholic entails. Again, I encourage you to ask questions about your faith, not to cause you to doubt your faith but rather to be sure you understand why we believe, what we believe as Catholics, and then to seek the answers to become knowledgeable, so you can better understand and thus strengthen your faith and credibly share your faith with others! You will be a better witness as a result!

So, now the answer please!!! Much of what Jesus said and did while on earth and most of what God inspired prophets and biblical authors to say and do were not principally meant for the ears of those that directly heard, or the first set of eyes that read the scriptural passages. God/Jesus, knew that all of scripture and all Jesus's acts and teachings would be reviewed, discussed and also challenged by generation after generation. Jesus said and did things intentionally to send us all very specific messages, many times in anticipation of how his message might be either intentionally (Pharisee types) or unintentionally misinterpreted.

Jesus is omniscient and was very much prepared for his mother to 'put him on the spot" and basically force him to start his public life. In fact, it was no accident his first miracle was at a wedding feast. Not only was he prepared for his mother's request, he planned it that way! Remember, we cannot always let the facts get in the way of a good story!! Meals are used throughout Sacred Scripture in parables and during real events (like the Wedding Feast at Cana) to make critical points or to deliver important church teachings or positions. Jesus knew meals would transcend time. You all know there were four key messages this story reveals to us: the sanctity of the marital covenant and God's covenant with his people; to prepare us for the ultimate feast, the Last Supper when he would transform wine into his blood (and bread into his body); to show us he can never refuse his mother, so pray to Mary to intercede on your behalf (remember we are not praying to Mary to directly answer our prayers); and, to officially mark the beginning of his public life.

Remember, everything Jesus said or did was for a purpose and with the full use of all his omniscient and omnipotent capabilities. There were no miscues, re-spins or retractions like those that are in vogue today with most politicians who let their mouth's get ahead of their brains. Some of our other Christian brothers have a hard time believing some of the subtler points the Church makes when interpreting scripture. They fail to appreciate every word spoken or inspired had a real and important meaning or purpose. This is one reason why I used so many examples in class regarding the problem with biblical translations, transliterations, or simplifications (or even children's bibles) of scripture. A slight deviation can profoundly affect the interpretation one might make from a scriptural passage. This is one reason why we rely on the Pope and the Magisterium who are well versed in the biblical languages, historical references, the cultural implications of what was said and not said, and most importantly, are the ones inspired by the Holy Spirit to ascertain the correct original message God intended to convey to us!

98. Why do we have to be a certain age to receive our First Communion Sacrament of the Holy Eucharist)?

The Sacrament of Holy Eucharist is the most sacred and special of all seven sacraments because it is the only sacrament that contains Christ himself while the other sacraments are "channels for receiving God's grace". To receive this sacrament at all we must be without mortal sin. Therefore, by default we must have already been baptized to remove original sin. To receive communion on a regular basis we must be without mortal sin (you need to be clear what these include, for one mortal sin young adults are most susceptible to is, missing mass on a Sunday or a Holy Day without a valid reason.

In your case, or at your age as eighth graders, you should make at least as much effort to have your parents get you to Sunday mass as you do to have them get you to athletic events/practices, school, parties and other extracurricular activities. If your parents won't take you or decline to take you on a given Sunday and, you cannot get there on your own (walk or take a bike), it is not a mortal sin for you. Also, you must have known that it was a sin. You may have known it was a sin, but you may not have known it was a mortal sin. Sorry but now you know!!).

Okay back to the question. The Church's position is you must be at the "age of discretion" or the "age of reason" which is generally determined to be the age of seven or eight. This is also the youngest age you could receive the sacrament of Confirmation. Each bishop (who confers the Sacrament of Confirmation) decides what age Confirmation will be offered in their diocese or for their "flock". You also should have received the sacrament of Reconciliation prior to your First Communion, so you can cleanse your soul of any sins. You therefore need to be old enough to understand the concept of right and wrong, know what the three conditions are for an act to be a sin (must know it is wrong, must commit the act of your own free will, or in the case of sins of omission, freely not do what you should have done, and lastly, actually commit the wrong act), and to be able to differentiate between mortal and venial sins, etc. You must also be truly sorry and committed to trying to do better in the future despite our human, weak natures. Lastly, you must be able to have some understanding of the Sacrament of the Holy Eucharist and the Real Presence of Christ in the Eucharist. This is a difficult concept for humans to grasp and requires a good degree of faith.

As Catholics we believe the bread and wine is changed, in substance (not in look, feel, smell or taste), that its very essence, is changed from ordinary food and drink into God's real body and blood. This is not light stuff, in fact, I would bet there are numerous Catholics out there today who do not either believe or fully understand Catholic dogma on this topic. So, for all these reasons and many more, we need to be old enough to grasp the basic elements of the Sacrament of Reconciliation and of Holy Eucharist before we can properly receive our First Communion. There has been much debate over what that age should be and arguably, it should not be the same for each one of us. Unlike angels whose intellects were fully developed upon their creation, we humans develop our intellects at different rates of speed or ages.

So, by now you wish I had given you the short answer… because the Magisterium of the Church says so!

99. Why do Protestants think it is wrong for Catholics to pray to Mary?

Some non-Catholics think we are idolizing or especially holding Mary up to be equal to God or to her son Jesus as the third person in the Trinity, especially if they think we are praying directly to Mary to answer our prayers or petitions as though she were a god. This is similar to the whole question of praying to saints or praying before statues or other icons, i.e. representations of Mary or the saints, "God-pointers" if you will. If we did hold Mary or the saints to be gods then we would be committing a sin against the first commandment, "I am the Lord thy God, thou shall not have strange gods/idols before me". There is a real difference between praying and worshiping. We Catholics are not praying to Mary or to the saints to answer our prayers and certainly we do not regard them as gods or equals to God. Rather we are praying to them to intercede on our behalf. We are asking Mary or the "Communion of Saints" to go to Jesus and ask him for us to hear and answer our prayers. Our protestant brothers would ask, why use a middleman? Why not go direct to Jesus? Of course, we could, and we do, but if we note the message of the Wedding Feast at Cana, we might want to try multiple approaches to petition God. Also, we might have a saint or two we particularly relate to by name or by a parallel of their life story to ours. For some of us, at varying times in our lives', there is comfort and even special graces related to praying to those saints (like the novena to St. Jude for hopeless or desperate cases or the Divine Mercy Chaplet) asking for intercession with Jesus on our behalf either in addition to or in lieu of praying directly to Jesus.

There are several related points which center around: the importance of prayer; having a relationship with Mary; the value of praying the Rosary; and, key things to remember about prayer. We learn from the Wedding feast at Cana in John's gospel, how Mary pointed out to her son Jesus, the bride's mother, ran out of wine to serve her guests. This was a real "faux pas" back in Jesus's time. Weddings back then could go on for days. You always served your best wine first and certainly never ran out. At the wedding in Cana the wine did run out! However, Jesus responded to his mother, when she pointed out the problem of the wine shortage, "what is this to me and to you woman and he goes on to say, "my hour has not yet come". Jesus is not being disrespectful to his mother. I explained in class the significance of his referring to his mother as gunae or woman was to remind us Mary is the woman promised by God in Genesis, who would come, and her seed would be the redeemer of the world and would triumph over evil/Satan.

However, what is also significant was that he was telling his mother his time had not come to begin to reveal himself to start his public life. However, Mary as Jesus's mother, turns to the servers and tells them to do whatever her son instructs them to do. In short, she is basically using her position as Jesus's mother to ask Jesus to do as she requests. Jesus cannot refuse his mother and so he begins his public life by performing his first miracle as reported in John's gospel to turn the water into wine. Which we also know is a precursor or a sign of the greater miracle to come at the Last Supper when he will turn wine into his precious blood.

The key point here is that the bride's mother is symbolic of us. If we petition Mary to intercede on our behalf to her son Jesus, to hear and answer our prayers, he cannot and will not refuse his mother. It is important to pray to Mary and to the particular saints we can relate closely to, not with the intent or expectation to answer our prayers directly, but rather to ask them to intercede or to go to Jesus on our behalf. For Jesus said, "knock and the door shall be open to you".

There is another point on prayer that is very important. When we pray, we should know that all our prayers are heard by God but may not be answered in the time frame we want, or we may not even know Jesus answered our prayers because he may not answer them exactly as we asked or expected him to. When we pray, we should strive to be balanced in our approach. We should not always be asking for things or lead with requests for help. Rather, we should balance requests for help with prayers of thanks for all we have already been blessed with. Also, we should always begin our prayer sessions acknowledging God's divine nature, his all forgiving nature, his all-powerful and all-knowing nature. We are acknowledging that if it is his will, he can grant our petition. We should also acknowledge that our desires or wills may not necessarily align with God's plan or will for us. We should always ask God for the grace and strength to know, accept and live our lives' according to his will for us, not according to our wills!

Jesus does hear and answer all our prayers but not necessarily in our time frames or in the exact way we asked him to. If I get the chance, I will share a real-life example from Randy Alcorn, a well-known Christian author, who went to Jesus with a special prayer request. God answered Randy's prayer, but it took Randy a few years to realize just how wonderfully God had answered his prayer. It took a while to unfold and become clear to him. It is important to realize God has an overall plan for each one of us and for this world. He also prepared a special place for each one of us in heaven for Jesus said, "Do not let your heart be troubled; believe in God, believe also in me. In my Father's house are many dwelling places; if it were not so, I would have told you; for I go to prepare a place for you. If I go and prepare a place for you, I will come again and receive you to myself, so that where I am, *there* you may be also" (Jn 14:1-3).

We cannot fully appreciate this plan and how individual circumstances fit with that overall plan. This is another reason why we must remain strong in our faith, in both good times and in bad times. We need to accept the good and the difficult as graces from God to help us on our journey to heaven. It is always easy for me to be in a good mood when I am playing well on the golf course. The real and harder test is whether I retain that positive mood when I am playing poorly. So, it is with our relationship with Jesus and the strength of our faith. Peter was very brave at the Last Supper but not later that evening when Jesus was arrested. It is not always easy to remain strong and faithful, especially in today's world! So, we pray to stay close to God, to develop a relationship with Him, and to remain open and accepting of his plan for us.

100. How do we Catholics know all the things we believe are true?

This is a very good and complex question. Again, books have been written on or around this question. So why should you as a developing Catholic believe that the Catholic Church has it all figured out? Why not some other Christian faith denomination or some other non-Christian faith??

First, we do not know, for a fact, that every aspect of the Catholic Church's position on every single article of faith is one hundred percent spot on. I could not prove, and I do not believe the Catholic Church could "prove" every point that would satisfy a court of law. This does not make these positions any less solid or valid. You must remember we are talking articles of faith. Webster's Collegiate Dictionary defines faith as "positions not fully supported by material evidence".

That said, there is preponderance of scriptural, historical and tradition-based evidence that is the cornerstone of Catholic dogma. When you combine all these pieces of evidence with the historical fact that there was a man named Jesus that many believed at that time based on his miracles, his words, and his actions (including historical evidence that he died and rose from the dead), that he was the Son of God, the Word Incarnate (the Word made flesh). For so many to believe in him Jesus would have to have been one of three things: a great liar who was able to fool thousands, crazy (for he proclaimed himself to be God) and yet no one took him for being crazy, or, he was who he proclaimed himself to be (please know this general observation put far more profoundly and was made famous by the great Christian writer, C.S. Lewis in his book, *Mere Christianity*).

Our Catholic beliefs flow from this core belief in Jesus Christ being exactly who he said he was. We believe, and scripture supports, that Jesus fulfilled the promises made in the Old Testament as part of his becoming man. We also believe Jesus established Peter as the head of his church and his fellow disciples as the first bishops and priests. He promised them he would be with them always and that the power of Satan would not prevail against them.

He did not promise they would be perfect, sinless and without error in terms of interpreting and applying scripture to our ever-changing world. He did promise to inspire them and to direct them through the help of the Holy Spirit. Remember when Peter responded to Jesus' question, "who do you say that I am? Peter proclaimed Jesus to be the Son of God, the Messiah promised in the Old Testament. Jesus, said to Peter, "you did not come to this knowledge on your own, rather you learned it from my Father" and then he made Peter the head of his Church. He was telling Peter, his disciples, and all of us, that God the Father would inspire the leaders of his Church, so they would know how to "shepherd his flock".

I contend that it would have made no sense for God the Father to send his Son to us, have him become fully man (while retaining his fully divine nature as well); let him dwell among us to expand our relationship with him; enable him to conquer sin and evil by allowing him to be subjected to torture and the worst form of death and then rise from the dead; only to then rise up to heaven leaving us, his church behind to "figure it out all on our own". Had he done this; he would have had far less foresight than the founding fathers of our country. They had the wisdom and foresight to create a new form of government that could bend and flex to our ever-changing world by creating a constitution with an amendment process and three branches of government to insure a balance of power and control.

Doesn't it make sense that the Son of God would have at least as much foresight and wisdom as our founding fathers??? Therefore, it is easy for me to accept that Jesus meant to make Peter and his successors the head of his Church and to put a structure or authoritative hierarchy and that he would bless them with special help/inspiration.

When you get older, I encourage you to read a book by Lee Strobel, *"The Case for the Real Jesus"*. Lee Strobel was a former Chicago Tribune writer who was also an atheist. He set out to research who this person known as Jesus really was as an objective reporter (however a reporter who did not believe in God and certainly did not believe Jesus was God). By the end of his years of research and countless interviews with numerous scholars from all faiths and those of no faith, people strongly pro, anti and with no definitive position on whether Jesus was who he claimed to be, Lee Strobel became a believer that Jesus did exist and that he was indeed the Son of God.

Pretty powerful! I cannot begin to fully answer your question as to how I know and believe the Church is the one true Church and why you should accept all its positions. Stay focused on the big picture, on the main points and live your life according to Jesus's teachings (The Great Commandment and the Beatitudes). If you do these well, to the very best of your ability, I firmly believe you will find eternal happiness in heaven with God.

101. How has God always been, doesn't everything have to have a beginning or starting point?

Most things do have a starting point, and an end point. That is, if we are talking about mortal beings, or humans or other earthly creatures and earthly objects (creations). Humans are born, and our human bodies eventually die. Plants and animals go through the same cycle. Our universe had a definite beginning point and will have a definite end point. Scientists have been able to measure a continual decrease in "energy" in the universe. How does this fit with our scientific notion that matter cannot be created or destroyed? I will explain.

When God introduced himself to Moses in the Old Testament, He did so by speaking to Moses in the form of fire in a burning bush (which was not actually burning even though it was on fire). When Moses asked who he was, God identified himself using the Hebrew word "Yahweh", which means" I am, who am". This means I am the one who always was, and parenthetically means, the one who always will be. God is a supreme being that always was and always will be. As a supreme being he is immortal, he does not have a physical nature that is subject to pain, hunger or death and is not bound by space, time, or matter. Many philosophers and scientists agree, aside from their various religious beliefs, that there had to be a God or a supreme being that always was to explain the origins of our universe and of man. The physical proof God is real is all around us in creation and in each other.

There are numerous excellent books that help us rationally deduce that there must be a God. Other arguments for the origin of the world and man such as the Big Bang Theory or Evolution Theory have at least one common and major flaw in terms of fully explaining the origin of our universe. I love the Big Bang Theory (which by the way was developed by a Catholic priest, Fr. Georges Lemaître) because it harmonizes with Catholic creation dogma, evolution theory and it solved a problem for Einstein's Theory of Relativity. Proponents of the Big Bang Theory agree that there was nothing and then suddenly there was this event, this explosion and then we had the universe, or the beginning point for the universe as we now know it.

So, while greatly simplified, this sounds just like Catholic Creation dogma. However, Big Bang theorists do not explain what caused the Big Bang, how and who created the matter that actually "banged", or who made the first life form that we evolved from. Furthermore, the "fine tuning", the order and complexity of our world, our universe, our human bodies, of all the numerous species we know of, etc., is a strong argument against a big bang that just randomly happened. This all argues for a more supremely ordered, designed or purposeful creation and plan. For more details on this, please see Fr. James Spitzer's Credible Catholic modules from the Magis Center.

In philosophical terms this is known as the First Cause. This First Cause had to be an "Uncaused, First Cause" that is, not limited by time, space or matter. So yes, matter cannot be created nor destroyed, at least not by mortal man, or humans, so it required a Supreme Being to make or create matter and start the process of creation or to be that First Cause. Also, we have thousands of historical, biblical and other examples of miracles that can only be attributed to God, to a Supreme Being. We as humans always want to have documented proof so we can feel better (to help us accept or understand the miracle). While this is normal, it is also a reflection of our human nature. We cannot begin to fully comprehend God's supreme, divine qualities. Therefore, we call our faith a "gift" from God. We have a responsibility to grow this faith by strengthening our understanding of how the Church has come to the position it has on all key areas that define Catholic dogma. However, in the end, there is no irrefutable proof that those teachings are right, that God exists, or that Jesus was the Son of God. These all require the special gift of faith.

102. Why is the Church repeatedly making changes to its services?

I assume you are referring to mass services versus other sacramental services and rites. It had been forty years since the last change that occurred just a few years ago to our Catholic mass services and these changes are minimal compared to the changes of forty years ago following Vatican Two. But change can be hard and disruptive to many. However, I guarantee all of us paid much more attention to what the priest was saying and what we said in response as we adapted to the new cannon of the mass. The Catholic Church is one of the oldest and longest running faiths with one of the largest followings for many very good reasons. One of them has been the consistency of Church dogma and its sacramental rites.

Your grandparents and their parents and their parents knew only a Latin form of mass where the priest's back was to the congregation. Vatican II changed this over forty years ago to an English translation of the Latin cannon and brought the Eucharistic table out and away from the wall so that the priest could stand and face the congregation on the other side of the altar and speak in a language their parishioners could understand.

This made the mass more meaningful and understandable to more people of all ages. This was first met with great resistance by many Catholics owing to how long we had the more traditional Latin mass and how we tend to resist major changes.

The most recent set of liturgical changes we learned to incorporate were designed to be truer to a more literal translation of the original Latin to English. It was felt back at the time of Vatican II that a stricter translation of the Latin cannon would have been too difficult for most people to get comfortable with given the degree of change they were already going to have to work through. So, they made the translation more "user friendly". Now forty years later, the Church has decided we are mature enough to return to a truer translation of the original Latin into English.

One of the reasons I have been saying a Latin sign of the cross during prayer in class instead of in English, is to help us think more about what we are doing and saying, with the hope that our prayers would be that much more meaningful. I hope this has happened to some extent and will continue to happen as you accept and incorporate the new translation of our mass liturgy into your regular mass participation experience.

I strongly encourage you to go to a church where they still offer a high (this means they sing most of the liturgy) Latin mass. Now that you are a regular attendee and participant at Sunday masses, it would be a wonderful experience to attend mass said and sung in Latin. Hopefully you will have an opportunity to experience a high Latin mass (ideally in a Cathedral) soon!

103. Is having sex before marriage a sin?

And someone else asked, "Why is it bad to have sex before marriage?"

The short answer to the first question is "yes". Fr. Hardon's, *The Question and Answer Catholic Catechism,* states on pages 149 and 150,

"The Church teaches that all non-marital sexual relations are a serious deviation from divine law. They have been forbidden to the followers of Christ since the beginning of Christianity.

> Non-marital sexual relations are sinful because the marital act is legitimate only within the bond of marriage. Intercourse without marriage is an untruth because it belies

the total commitment to one another that the marital act expresses between husband and wife. Intercourse without marriage is also an injustice to the children that may be conceived, since they would lack the dignity, stability, security, and loving care that marriage is expected to provide."

For a different but aligned answer to your second question, look up question #162 in Matthew J. Pinto's, *Did Adam & Eve Have Belly Buttons?* He reminds us God invented sex and as such it is a good thing. However, with all good things there comes certain responsibilities. Why? Because God does not want the good thing to be a source of pain, evil selfishness or death. He wants sexual relations, between a man and a woman (not people of the same sex), to be the absolutely profound and wonderful act it was meant to be. He gave us the sexual attraction to bring the two sexes together in a way that would lead to the marriage covenant and to procreation, which is the ultimate (not the only) purpose of marriage.

In addition to the above explanation, for the person who asked the second question I noted above, I strongly encourage you to read the answer to question 165 in this same book by Matthew Pinto. The answer gives the fifteen reasons why you should not have premarital sex! Great reasons and great logic behind each one of them, many of which have nothing to do with your Catholic faith and yet are consistent with the Church's thinking!

104. Why do we have a Pope?

We have a Pope because Jesus believed that for our salvation, and to insure his Church would never die here on earth, we would need a leader that could, with the help of the other disciples, (now the bishops, or the teaching body of the Church known as the Magisterium) and the help of the Holy Spirit, continually apply Jesus's teachings, his message, to our ever-changing world. I believe Jesus is at least as smart and as forward thinking as the forefathers of our great country. Our forefathers, when we won our independence from England, created a constitution and three branches of government that could lead and help insure the long-term future of our country. In short, our forefathers created a structural foundation that was solid but also had built-in "tools" or vehicles to flex to changing conditions that became the bedrock of our country. Jesus did the same thing when he made Peter, "the Rock" upon which he built his Church.

In John 21:6-17 when Jesus appeared to the disciples while they were fishing after his Resurrection, Jesus asks Peter three times if Peter loved him. After each affirmation of Peter's love, Jesus said "feed my sheep". This was Jesus's way of reaffirming that Peter was to be the first head of his church here on earth. This was a validation of Jesus's faith and confidence in Peter despite Peter having denied Jesus three times. Jesus had earlier promised Peter that upon him he would build his Church (Mt 16:13-19).

Also, Jesus warned Peter at the Last Supper that, "Satan has received permission to test all of you to separate the good from the bad as a farmer separates the wheat from the chafe. But I have prayed for you Simon that your faith will not fail. And when you turn back to me, you must strengthen your brothers" (Lk 22:31-32). Note that Jesus refers to Peter in this passage by his old name of Simon when he predicts Peter (Simon) will turn away from him. However, Jesus predicts Peter's return to faith in Jesus and he promises to pray for Peter and then Peter is to use that grace and strength to strengthen his "brothers". They all turned from Jesus, but Jesus only promised to pray for Peter and then Peter was to help the others. Jesus knew that our world would continue to change and evolve, and he wanted to provide a structure that would enable his Church to grow an evolve based on the messages he intended for us to know, understand and to apply, as he showed us through his life here on earth, and through the inspired words of the various biblical authors. His message does not change, there are no new revelations. What does change is how we apply his intended messages to this ever-changing world.

105. If someone asks me "What does it mean to be Catholic?", what do I say?

Much depends on who is asking you, why you think they are asking the question, how well you know them, and, how well they know and trust you. The depth and tone of your answer should be a function of all of these as you want to satisfy and encourage the curious, those that might truly be seeking, without pouring out all you know about your Catholic faith on them. You do not want them "drinking from a fire hose" but you want to answer with conviction and in a manner that will encourage them to want to hear more.

You could begin with an "elevator pitch" based on the kerygma but without referencing it as such! Many Catholics are not familiar with the term *kerygma*, and so they can be perplexed when they see or hear it, let alone someone not familiar with the Catholic faith or Christianity. *Kerygma* is a Greek term that basically means "preaching" and is used to describe the content of the apostolic message of Jesus. St. Paul reminds us in Romans 10:14 that preaching is essential for people to believe in Jesus and to be saved. When Paul referred to preaching the *kerygma*, he was referring to a very specific message, not just a general homily on any aspect of faith. Paul preached first and foremost the message of Jesus's death and resurrection and their related saving significance for each one of us. Paul also preached on the response required of us to accept and live out this saving action of Jesus.

The content of Paul's preaching may seem simple, but it should be understood as the foundation upon which everything else is based. All other Christian teaching depends on and flows from the truth of our Lord's saving death and resurrection.

To understand the impact of St. Paul's preaching, we must place it in the context of the larger story of salvation. It is important to remember God created the world, and it was good, and he intended humanity to live with him in a communion of peace and love. This original state of grace was lost through disobedience which disrupted our communion with God and others and resulted in a state of alienation and disharmony (the fall). God's original plan for our lives was obscured by the darkness of sin. Humanity was in a fallen state from which we could not save ourselves.

In the fullness of time, God sent his only Son, Jesus Christ, to be our Savior from the forces of sin and death. Jesus restored our right relationship with God the Father through the reconciliation (peace) of his cross. He opened the gates of heaven to us through his resurrection and ascension. Jesus reigns eternally as Lord of heaven and earth with the Father and the Holy Spirit. Moreover, he has sent his Holy Spirit into our hearts so that we can be formed as part of his mystical body in the communion of the church where he continues to speak his word to us and to feed us with his very self (body and blood) in the Eucharist.

The forces of sin and death no longer have the last word for those who accept and respond to what Jesus has done for us in God's plan of salvation. Rather, Christians who share fully in the life of grace are drawn deeply into an eternal communion of life and love with the Father, through the Son, and in the Holy Spirit.

That's a very powerful message! And it is a message we must accept and respond to. We as Catholics accept and experience that message through the sacraments, especially Baptism. We regularly accept that message through the profession of the Creed and the reception of the Holy Eucharist at mass. Saying "Yes" to the message of Jesus's death and resurrection reorients our entire life in every possible way. This reorientation of life is called conversion. Responding to the message of Jesus's death and resurrection can be challenging because there are enormous implications for our lives, which Paul speaks well about in his letters to the early Christians.

Accepting and responding to a new life in the "Risen Christ" has moral implications as we are called to live as "Children of God". Accepting and responding to the Lordship of Jesus means that we seek and follow God's guidance in every decision. Living in the communion of the Holy Spirit as the body of Christ, means we are active members of the Church who celebrate our Lord in word and sacrament and become his presence in the world as missionary disciples.

However, I appreciate this kerygmatic based response may be way too much for you or them, especially as an initial response to a slightly curious person, so you might begin by simply telling them that as a Catholic you are first a Christian which means you believe Jesus is the Son of God made flesh and that he was crucified, he died, was buried, rose from the dead on the third day and then ascended into heaven. Also, that through his death and resurrection he conquered sin and death, so we could ultimately be happy with him in heaven upon our death or on the Final Judgement Day. But again, even this by be way too much, you must relate to the person asking, you have to be a friend to them first and only provide enough of a response to pique their curiosity, to invite or encourage future dialog.

As a Catholic, we believe the Catholic Church is the one true Church instituted by Jesus Christ with Peter as the first Pope or leader and with the other apostles as the first bishops/priests. However, we do not believe Catholic's have an exclusive on heaven. We believe non-Catholics and non-Christians all have an opportunity to enjoy eternal life in heaven but would argue living according to the Catholic faith provides the best, highest probable path to getting there. I address this more deeply in response to other questions in this book.

Since the question focused specifically on the Catholic faith, you could go on to explain (but probably in a future or follow-up discussion, for remember, you don't want to come on too heavy, especially early on. As I said, you want to be inviting and welcoming while fueling their curiosity.) that there are several doctrines that we accept and believe in that our Christian brothers do not accept, and no other religious faith denominations believe either, so there are doctrines that are more unique to our Catholic faith. Some of these include but are not limited to: The Real Presence of Christ in the Eucharist; The Immaculate Conception of Mary; Mary's virgin birth of Jesus, the Assumption of Mary body and soul into heaven; that Jesus made Peter and all of his successors the head of the Catholic Church on earth, and that the Pope is infallible on matters of dogma when he speaks "ex cathedra", or "from the throne"; in the Communion of Saints, that we can pray to intercede on our behalf...etc. In the end, this is not a question one can answer in a few minutes in one simple conversation, but it does open the door to leading the questioner to faith and relationship with Jesus. I maintain that the first priority is to help bring people into relationship with Jesus Christ as the Son of God and then help them come to know and love the fullness of Catholicism. Once they begin dialog in real interest, you can continue to build upon and feed their curiosity.

106. How can Jesus be the Son of God and also the son of God's daughter Mary?

Good, thoughtful question! However, you are asking me to explain the mystery of the Trinity. Trinitarian doctrine is very difficult to explain yet alone wrap our heads around, but all Christian faiths believe in Trinitarian doctrine.

The short answer is God the Father, through the Holy Spirit, is responsible for Jesus's divine nature in the person we know as Jesus. We believe Jesus was simultaneously wholly divine (or wholly God) and wholly man (human). Mary is responsible for Jesus's human nature. As a result, Jesus was both the Son of the Holy Spirit (through the power of God the Father) and the son of Mary. This is why we say Mary's relationship to the Trinity is that she is the daughter of God the Father; the spouse of the Holy Spirit; and the Mother of God the Son.

107. Will you go to hell if you are a soldier and need to kill people to defend our country?

The short answer is no. The Church's position on war is that this is a matter of state. The Church is not for or against war. However, the Church strongly encourages leaders of nations to pursue all possible courses of resolving disputes via diplomatic means. If, as you say, in order to defend themselves from aggressors, and after vigorously working all diplomatic avenues, a country's leaders decide that war is necessary, the Church strongly encourages the battle be waged in a manner that focuses on army against army and not on innocent civilians. They strongly encourage government leaders to avoid the use of weaponry that mass destroys and kills indiscriminately. Read Fr. John A. Hardon's, *The Catholic Catechism,* pages 234-235 for answers on this and related questions about war.

108. How should I choose the best Confirmation saint name for me?

This a good question for sometimes Confirmation saint's names are chosen because they sound cool or blend well with the rest of our name or for other similar "soft" reasons. You should spend time researching saint's backgrounds and try to find a saint with whom you can readily identify with or more closely relate to. Maybe they chose a vocation or a path in life that feels right or is similar to a calling you may be feeling. Maybe their life story serves as a model or inspiration for you. Their courage, conviction or circumstances may have a special meaning to you. The more saints you research, the more likely one will stand out as being the right one for you.

Another option would be to pick the name of a person who today is a strong role model for you (this is also how you should select your Confirmation sponsor, but your saint name and sponsor name certainly can be very separate choices). Be sure it is an actual saint name that you pick although it can be a derivative of a saint's name. This process will also open your eyes, and hopefully your heart, to committing yourself to doing kind acts, to regularly committing some of your time and talents to doing some form of community service through the help and intercession of your Confirmation saint. This is how you live your faith. Hopefully your research of these devoted humans inspires you to model your life after their saintly ways. The name you pick should be a source of that inspiration.

109. What does it meant to be Confirmed? How are we different as a result?

First, Confirmation is one of the seven sacraments in the Catholic Church and is one of three "Sacraments of Initiation" (Baptism and Holy Eucharist are the other two). Sacraments are outward signs instituted by Christ to provide sanctifying grace.

When you were baptized (assuming this happened shortly after you were born, versus going through an adult formation program later in life) your parents spoke on your behalf and accepted Jesus Christ as your Lord and Savior for you. Now you, essentially complete what was started in baptism. Too many candidates for the Sacrament of Confirmation think of this as a sort of "graduation" or a completion of their faith journey. This could not be further from the truth. In fact, it is exactly the opposite. It is a new beginning. Through the Sacrament of Confirmation, you are fully initiated into the Catholic Church. Confirmation is only a graduation in the sense that as the third Sacrament of Initiation you have completed the formal initiation process into the Catholic Church. One is initiated into something not as an ending but as a beginning, as a full-fledged member with all its' attendant rights, privileges and obligations.

When you are confirmed, you receive special grace from the Holy Spirit that effectively seals this initiation; strengthens you to continue your faith journey; draws you closer to Christ; and enables you to evangelize, to help draw others to the Catholic faith you are now fully initiated into. As part of your Confirmation you are committing to deepening your relationship with Christ, to live your life consistent with the teachings of the Catholic Church and to profess your faith to others. In other words, you are committing to help bring others to Christ.

Popular society today tells us our faith and our beliefs are relative, that there are no absolute truths and that we should keep our faith to ourselves. This is not what Jesus taught. He gave us the gift, the most wonderful gift of himself and the opportunity for eternal salvation through his sacrifice of persecution, crucifixion, death and resurrection. This is a gift he told us to go out and share with all we encounter. We can do this through our everyday thoughts, prayers, words and actions. At Confirmation, we are infused with the same gifts, fruits and graces of the Holy Spirit the apostles received on Pentecost. Our challenge is to leverage these gifts based on our individual daily opportunities and unique charisms we received at baptism.

Learning about your faith and developing a personal relationship with Jesus is a never-ending process. When you commit to and receive, the acrament of Confirmation, you will not only be committing yourself and your life to God and the service of others, but you are also saying you accept the teachings of the Catholic Church and agree to continue developing a deeper understanding of your faith. Your parents committed for you at your baptism. Now you are standing up and saying, "I believe" and "I will actively live my life in a manner consistent with those beliefs. I will be an active witness or disciple of my Catholic faith." You can now tell other Christians you have accepted Jesus Christ as your Lord and Savior. However, as a confirmed Catholic you are also recognizing that saying it is not enough! As St. James said, "Faith without works is dead." While we cannot make up for our sinful natures' or earn our way into heaven by doing good deeds, we cannot just "say" we accept Jesus as our personal Lord and Savior without also living consistent with that belief!

Confirmation, at least in the vernacular of the Catholic Church and as a

Sacrament of Initiation primarily means to strengthen and to witness. We know this sacrament today to be a time for those who have been baptized (a pre-requisite to Confirmation), to re-affirm their belief or their acceptance of their Catholic baptismal promise to be a follower of Christ. Secondly, it requires a commitment to take on a more important role as a witness or as an advocate of Christ. To do this effectively one must deepen one's knowledge of his or her faith and relationship with Christ. Confirmation is a commitment to take both these courses of action.

Fr. Hardon's The Catholic Catechism on page 518, reminds us:

> Confirmation increases the persons possession of divine
> life; it confers actual graces and what is called the special

sacramental grace peculiar to this sacrament; and, in this case, it also gives a unique sacramental character" defined in four unique forms:

1. The person who is confirmed receives a deepening of God's friendship and, as we commonly say, an increase in sanctifying grace. Since the state of grace means a share in the life of God, we should expect this sacrament to affect that area of divine life which has to do with the capacity to survive. Thus, the supernatural life becomes more resilient, more capable of resisting dangers to its continued existence and growth, and to be more alert to protecting itself against what might threaten its well-being.

2. Actual graces as illuminations of the mind and inspirations of the will to meet the needs of the spiritual life, are also received. The sacrament confers these graces "by title," for those who are confirmed before the age of reason, and both actually and "by title" for persons who receive the sacrament after the age of discretion. The difference between these two forms of obtaining grace is simply that the confirmed Christian is gifted with additional helps from God to live out his faith courageously, and he receives the help not only at the moment of confirmation, but also acquires a claim or a title to such divine assistance for the rest of his life, as occasion and circumstances require.

3. This special sacramental grace is to perfect, in the sense of complete, the effects of baptism. It brings to perfection the supernatural life infused at baptism by giving it the power to withstand opposition from within, which is human respect and fear, and from without, which is physical or psychological coercion to deny or compromise what the faith demands....

Vincent J. Heaton Jr.

We might say that the Sacrament of Confirmation enables the Christian to live up to Christ's mandate of taking up one's cross daily and following him faithfully, despite one's personal feelings and in the face of criticism or contradiction from others.

4. Confirmation also imprints a character on the soul of the Christian. This character means assimilation to Christ the priest, in the twofold sense of having the strength to bear suffering (passively) in union with him and the courage to sacrifice pleasant things (actively) out of love for him.

So, what are you after you are confirmed? You are a witness, a disciple, and a soldier for Christ. No longer will it be enough to just attend mass on Sunday's and to follow the Ten Commandments. Your responsibilities as a practicing Catholic go much further. You need to live your faith every day and love others as Jesus Christ loves us…every day. You also have a responsibility (this responsibility grows as you mature in age and in your faith) to spread Jesus's word to others. You are to share the "Good News". You can do this best by how you live your life. What I mean is that the first Christians became so because either Jesus or one of his disciples spoke to them and shared the "Good News" with them. This is what we are all called to do as confirmed Catholics!

Resources

This is list of published books, audio books, presentations and on-line resources are referenced or mentioned in this book.

1. *The Catholic Bible*. New American Bible, Personal Study Edition, Oxford: University Press, 1995.
2. *Catechism of the Catholic Church*. 2nd ed. Washington D.C.: United States Catholic Conference, Inc., Liberia Editrice Vaticana, 1994.
3. Hardon, John A. *S.J., The Catholic Catechism*. New York: Doubleday, Division of Bantam Doubleday Dell Publishing Group, Inc., 1981.
4. Hardon, John A. *S.J., The Question and Answer Catholic Catechism*. New York: Doubleday, Division of Bantam Doubleday Dell Publishing Group, Inc., 1981.
5. Alcorn, Randy. *In Light of Eternity of Eternity*. Colorado Springs, CO: Waterbrook Press, a division of Random House, Inc., 1999
6. Alcorn, Randy. *If God is Good*. New York: Waterbrook Multnomah, a division of Random House, Inc.
7. Lewis, C.S. *Mere Christianity*. HarperCollins Publishers, 1952
8. Pinto, Matthew J,. *Did Adam & Eve Have Belly Buttons?*. West Chester, PA: Ascension Press, LLC, 1998.
9. Welborn, Amy. *Prove It!*. Huntington, IN: Our Sunday Visitor Publishing division, Our Sunday Visitor, Inc., 2001.
10. Strobel, Lee. *The Case For The Real Jesus*. Grand Rapids, MI: Zondervan, 2007.
11. Johnson, Timothy Luke. *The Great Courses*. Recorded Book, Emory University, The Teaching Company.

12. Spitzer, Fr. Robert J,. *Credible Catholic.* On-line Modules at https://www.crediblecatholic.com/programs/ Garden Grove, CA: The Magis Center, 2017.

13. Pennock, Matthew Francis. *What We Really Want to Know. Notre Dame, IN:* Ave Maria Press, Inc., 1996.

14. West, Christopher. *Theology of the Body for Beginners.* Ascension Press, 2009.

15. Evert, Jason. *Theology of the Body for Teens.* West Chester,_PA: Ascension Press, LLC, 2016.

16. Evert, Jason. *Saint John Paul the Great.* Ignatius Press, 2014

17. Anderson, Joan Wester. *Where Angels Walk.* New York: Ballentine Books, a division of Random House Inc., 1992.

18. Idleman, Kyle. *Not a Fan.* Grand Rapids, MI: Zondervan, 2011.

19. Strohm, Keith. Deacon, Archdiocese of Chicago, *Discipleship Formation Course. 2018*

Index

About the Author

Vince Heaton has been a Religious Education Catechist for over three decades focusing on preparing young adults for the Sacrament of Confirmation. He has also hosted joint parent/student sessions on the compatibility of science and religion and the scientific evidence supporting key Catholic doctrine based on the Magis Center's *Credible Catholic* modules. Vince has been a strong leader in his parish of St. Michael in Wheaton, IL and is one of fifteen children, with seven children and thirteen grandchildren of his own. He is committed to being a true disciple of Jesus Christ…spreading the "Good News"…and in his case…he uses many words…but most of them are very good ones!

Printed in the United States
By Bookmasters